The Unique Function of Education in American Democracy

Educational Policies Commission

National Education Association of the United States and the Department of Superintendence, 1201 Sixteenth Street, N. W., Washington, D. C.

Copyright, 1937
NATIONAL EDUCATION ASSOCIATION OF THE UNITED STATES
Washington, D. C.

———

First printing, February 1937
Second printing, April 1937
Third printing, October 1937

Acknowledgment

IN presenting this statement to the profession of education and to the general public, the Educational Policies Commission wishes to acknowledge its very great indebtedness to DR. CHARLES A. BEARD. When approaching the problem, the Commission decided to seek assistance from the man best qualified for the task by scholarship, social insight, and devotion to democratic institutions. The Commission thereupon voted without difficulty and with complete unanimity that Dr. Beard was specially fitted for this task. After several exploratory conferences with a subcommittee and a meeting with the Commission as a whole in August 1936, Dr. Beard prepared the first draft of the report contained in this volume. This draft was distributed to members of the Commission and a revision was made in the light of their comments. A second draft was discussed, amended, and approved for publication by the Commission in December 1936.

The Educational Policies Commission

Appointed by the National Education Association of the
United States and the Department of Superintendence

Appointed Members

ALEXANDER J. STODDARD, *Chairman*

CORNELIA S. ADAIR

LOTUS D. COFFMAN

GEORGE S. COUNTS

J. B. EDMONSON

FREDERICK M. HUNTER

CHARLES H. JUDD

JOHN K. NORTON

AGNES SAMUELSON

JOHN A. SEXSON

PAYSON SMITH

GEORGE D. STRAYER

WILLIS A. SUTTON

Ex-Officio Members

WILLARD E. GIVENS

ORVILLE C. PRATT

S. D. SHANKLAND

ALBERT M. SHAW

A. L. THRELKELD

Advisory Members

J. W. STUDEBAKER

GEORGE F. ZOOK

———

William G. Carr, *Secretary*
1201 Sixteenth Street, N. W.
Washington, D. C.

Table of Contents

The Commission has been fortunate
in persuading
DR. HENDRIK WILLEM VAN LOON
to prepare the illustrations for
this volume

The Unique Function of Education in American Democracy

I.

CIRCUMSTANCES CALL UPON EDUCATIONAL LEADERSHIP TO RECONSIDER ITS POSITION AND OBLIGATIONS IN SOCIETY

THE mariner blown out of his course by adverse winds and sailing long under clouded heavens among dangerous reefs seizes the first opportunity to get his bearings and chart his way by fixed marks of sky or land. Likewise in the management of human affairs, although the analogy is not exact, it is often necessary for leaders of State, the professions, and callings, amid great disturbances, to take their reckonings—to recur to first principles. This applies to education as well as to other branches of national interest and activity. None is independent of the others. None occupies a position of impregnable security which permits it to escape the strains in domestic or foreign affairs.

The World War Profoundly Disturbed the Social Order of 1914.

Concerning the gravity of the disturbances that now call for reckonings there can be no doubt. Since the outbreak of the World War in 1914, American society has faced disconcerting issues of life at home and abroad, has experienced storms of passion, and encountered the vicissitudes of a profound economic dislocation. The human and economic destruction of the war itself, the ensuing overthrow of governments and social systems in Europe, the collapse of prosperity in the United States, and the jars of the depression have shaken American thought and practice from center to circumference.

But the Origins of Many Difficulties Lie Deeper than Military and Depression Events.

The disarrangement of contemporary affairs, however, cannot be ascribed solely to the explosions of the World War or to the business depression. The war and the economic crisis accentuated the problems of the schools and added new cares to old burdens; but distracting issues had appeared in education before these disturbances arose. Their origins lie deeper than military events and economic stringency, and they will not be automatically settled by a guarantee of peace or a return of prosperity. Indeed, apart from immediate distresses, the chief effect of the financial shortage has been to make the teaching profession and the interested public acutely aware of challenges and claims that had been dimly discerned years before the war and the panic broke in upon "the normal course of history."

The Mechanization and Urbanization of Economy Had Already Raised Problems.

An illustration or two will suffice, at this point, to indicate the nature of these exigencies long in process of development. Perhaps most insistent of all has been the economic shift induced by the spread of science and machinery into every section of the country, into agriculture as well as manufacturing. This shift created a demand for the most diversified technical training. It did more. By transforming the structure of the family, it rendered that ancient institution less able to discharge its historic obligations—intellectual, moral, and social. As the age limit for the employment of youth in industries was raised, millions of boys and girls were excluded by law from occupations once open to them. Likewise disruptive was the evident inability of industry to provide full employment for youth even at the legal age; as a result of many forces millions of young people ready and eager to enter upon a life work were denied the opportunity.

Society Had Begun To Shift Heavy
Burdens to the Schools.

With the mechanization and urbanization of economy, the American people confronted social conditions foreign to their earlier experience, and they made new demands upon the schools. Whether it was a matter of moral unrest among youth, crime, disease, or inebriety, they turned to the schools for aid, and imposed upon them obligations once assumed by the family and business and agriculture. It is scarcely going beyond the mark to say that American adults, somewhat stunned and baffled by the difficulties which their own activities had created, began to shift to the public schools the burdens of coping with them. The war and the depression merely underlined these problems. And there is no ground in experience for believing that a return to what is called prosperity will automatically solve them or remove them from consideration. They had been long in development. They had long carried with them intellectual, moral, and social obligations of the most perplexing nature. Efforts to deal with them now call for great resources of mind and spirit. The

[3]

challenges they present are in truth so fundamental as to be startling. Their very urgency is appalling to educators who fearlessly and courageously face the realities of contemporary life.

*Yet Education Operates Largely Within the Frame
of Earlier Conceptions of Social Needs.*

Although educational leadership has not been indifferent to the sharp thrusts of this revolution in American affairs, it has continued to operate largely within the conceptions of society which were formulated long before the close of the nineteenth century. For two generations that leadership has been assumed by professional educators, philosophers, and psychologists, and in the main it has taken for granted the security of the educational establishment and the very society which sustains it. Leaders have deepened, systematized, and implemented the thought of the pathbreakers, but they have not recast that thought in terms of the changed cultural setting. In this there is no special criticism of education, any more than of the other professions such as law and medicine. It is merely a fact that now invites thorough consideration.

*So Adjustment to Contemporary Conditions
and Opportunities Becomes Imperative.*

Such, in brief, are the events of recent years that call for an exploration and restatement of educational purposes and obligations. The order of things prevailing in 1914 or 1900 or 1895 cannot be recovered, any more than old age can recover its youth. To proceed on the assumption that it can be restored or will be restored by nature or some other mysterious process is to sacrifice knowledge to illusion or to the desire for an escape from responsibilities. It is in the living present, with things as they are, with time forever irreversible, that the bearings of education must be taken and its future charted.

This Adjustment Must Be Made in the
Terms of Public Interest.

The answer of education to this summons cannot be made merely in the technical language of the profession, although the imperatives of the profession must be respected. It cannot be given simply in camera, in secret committee. It must be made in full public view and in the terms of the society which education serves, as well as in its own terms. Not for the thoughtless and heedless, to be sure, is the statement to be formulated; but for that large and influential body of citizens who can distinguish between the enduring values of life and the distempers of immediate difficulties, political and economic. Yet no citizens of the Republic can be left out of the reckoning, for the welfare of all is involved in both the program of education and its application.

The Center of Observation Is in Society,
Not Merely in the Educational Profession.

It is not enough, therefore, to fix attention on professional conceptions of education alone. Observations must also be taken from the center of society, for education, government, economy, and culture are parts of the same thing. Hence a paradox. If educators are to make wide and real the reach of their theory and practice, they must step over the boundaries drawn by their profession and consider the unity of things. By concentrating affections on their sphere of special interest, they will separate education from the living body of society. Important as are the methods and procedures of education, they are means, not ends; and the ends themselves are linked with the genius, spirit, and purposes of the society in which education functions, by which it is sustained, vitalized, and protected. Yet in stepping over the boundaries of their profession to find their bearings, educators are at the same time compelled, by the nature of their obligations, to hold fast to those values of education which endure amid the changes and exigencies of society.

Five Guiding Principles Control
Our Exploration.

With the challenge of affairs, public and private, so urgent, what are the bearings by which to discover our position and chart our course? To what principles must we refer in discovering the task of education in American democracy? Five seem imperative.

1. Public education is anchored in the history of American civilization and at any given moment operates within the accumulated heritage of that civilization.

2. Every system of thought and practice in education is formulated with some reference to the ideas and interests dominant or widely cherished in society at the time of its formulation.

3. Once created and systematized, any program of educational thought and practice takes on professional and institutional stereotypes, and tends to outlast even profound changes in the society in which it assumed its original shape.

[6]

4. Any restatement of educational objectives and responsibilities which is rooted in reality takes into account the nature of professional obligations and makes adjustments to cope with the major changes wrought in society since the last general reckoning in education.

5. Any statement of educational objectives and responsibilities that is not merely theoretical involves a quest for the institutional forms and operating practices through which education can best attain its ends.

II.

The Founders of the Republic Exalted Education as a National Interest.

It is out of the historical development of American society that have come the ideas, aspirations, knowledge, and working rules which prevail today and set the task of education. There have been borrowings, of course. Beyond the founding of the Republic lies a vast background embracing the culture of antiquity, the Middle Ages, the Renaissance, and modern Europe. From this plenitude of resources American civilization has been enriched. But all that has been drawn from other times and places has been worked into the American heritage. Additional drafts may be made upon other nations in days to come. Research will bring new knowledge. Experiments may confirm new methods. Novel ideas may bid for favor. The spirit of inquiry and invention may be active. The aspirations of the living will be stirred by the eternal surge of the human heart. Even so, the past, distant and near, has given us our society, including all the material, intellectual, and moral manifestations with which education must work.

Its Development Falls into Three Broad Periods.

Judged by outstanding characteristics of policy and economy the history of this heritage in the United States falls into three general periods. The first extended from the establishment of the Republic to the advent of Jacksonian democracy. The second had a longer reach—from the inauguration of Andrew Jackson in 1829 to the eve of the World War. The third covers the years since the coming of that cataclysm. To be sure, no sharp division separates these periods; the fixing of exact dates is an arbitrary action, and is accompanied by a warning against accepting them as more than conveniences. Nor were the features of the first age all destroyed in the second, or the features of the first and second in the third. There have been siftings and accumulations, borrowings and modifications, survivals and mergers, now incorporated in American society, the heritage with which we work today.

The Republic Was Founded in an Age of High Tension.

The independence of America was established by revolution and war, accompanied by inevitable concentration, storm, and stress. America had broken with the past in many respects and had founded government on a new base—social purpose as distinguished from the prescriptive rights of class. It was an infant republic in a world of warring monarchies. Its leaders were searching for ways and means of ensuring the perpetuity of government so conceived, developing natural resources, applying the technical arts, and realizing a better life for the free members of society.

Founders of the Republic Laid Stress on the Public Interest.

The founders of the American Republic were concerned with more than the material aspects of life—with more than the exploitation of natural resources, the pursuit of private interests, and the enrichment of individuals. They were public personages embued with a deep sense of social responsibility. They had staked their lives and their fortunes on independence and the security of the Republic. They had devoted time, energies, and talents to the public interest, waging war against a foreign foe and against greed and passions in their own midst. With justice does a biographer of Washington say: "Excluding his boyhood, there were but seven years of his life in which he was not engaged in the public service."

The early leaders did not subscribe to the economic theory that the pursuit of private gain would automatically bring about the establishment of independence, the creation of a constitution, or the security and prosperity of the American nation. In fact, during the Revolution they had seen gambling in goods and securities almost wreck their cause. After victory had been won they saw emphasis on personal and sectional interests threaten the Union with dissolution. They knew from bitter experience that devotion to the public good and self-denial in private matters were necessary to the achievement of great social ends. Having risked their all in the creation of a nation, the ablest among them gave unremitting attention to the study of public affairs and the methods calculated to preserve and improve the independent society which their labors had brought forth.

The Idea of Government by a Fixed Special Interest Was Rejected.

It is true that many extremists relied heavily upon the ancient weapon of statecraft—force—for the assurance of social order, and looked upon government as an instrument of private advantage. They would have entrenched great wealth in politics by the establishment of high property qualifications on voting and office-holding. They would have given life terms to Presidents and Senators, and restricted popular participation in public affairs to the smallest possible limits. They would have permanently established a class government—government by "the rich and well-born," and were largely indifferent to popular culture and education. But this faction, though influential, was challenged by events. The verdict of the majority finally ran against it. The verdict of history condemned it. In the course of years the government established by the founders of the Republic came to rest on a wide popular base; and with the passing of time that base was broadened by constitutional enactments and political practices.

The Democratic Idea
Was Accepted.

In fact there was in the United States no aristocracy buttressed by special privileges in public law to provide support for a monarchy or an oligarchy. In the long run the fate of government and society had to be entrusted to the wisdom and knowledge of a widening mass of people. Some Americans accepted that fate with a wry face, but made the best of it. Others greeted it as a fulfilment of the principles proclaimed in the Declaration of Independence, and as marking a humane departure from the despotisms of Europe. This document had asserted that all men are created equal, and endowed by their Creator with certain inalienable rights, including life, liberty, and the pursuit of happiness; that governments derive their just powers from the consent of the governed; and that the people have the right to alter or abolish any form of government which becomes destructive of these ends. Lifted up against the background of European societies founded on force and prescriptive privileges, these were revolutionary doctrines. The future was to decide whether any government so conceived and so dedicated could long endure.

Cultural Responsibilities Were
Imposed on Government.

Concerning the responsibilities of government in matters of economy and culture, leaders of the Republic had equally positive convictions. They did not conceive government as founded on sheer force and confined to the punishment of criminals. If doubts arise respecting this matter, they can be resolved by reading President Washington's first inaugural address and his first message to Congress. In assuming his duties he declared that the preeminence of free government must be "exemplified by all the attributes which can win the affections of its citizens and command the respect of the world." While recognizing the place of force in national defense and the maintenance of government, he commended to Congress "the advancement of agriculture, commerce, and manufactures by all proper means," and the promotion of science, literature, and education. In taking this broad view of statesmanship, Washington was profoundly moved by the challenge of the occasion, for he said: "The preservation of the sacred fire of liberty and the destiny of the republican model of government are justly considered, perhaps, as *deeply*, as *finally* staked on the experiment entrusted to the hands of the American people."

The Vital Relation of Education to the
Social Order Was Recognized.

Having committed themselves to government by popular verdict, to a government with high social responsibilities, many founders of the American Republic turned to education as a guarantee that a government of this type would endure—not merely to political education narrowly adapted to the genius of American institutions, but to education in the arts, sciences, and letters, assuring a deeper foundation in civilization itself. If a contemporary, Samuel Blodget, is to be believed, the idea of establishing a national institution of learning was taken up with General Washington in 1775, while Revolutionary soldiers were quartered in buildings on the campus of Harvard College, and Washington then and there approved the idea.[1]

American Leaders Turned to Educational Planning.

However that may be, it is certain that shortly after independence was gained, many of the best minds in America began to draft comprehensive plans for systems of universal education, crowned by a national university. Among them was Dr. Benjamin Rush, physician, surgeon-general during the Revolutionary War, member of the Continental Congress, signer of the Declaration of Independence, and member of the Pennsylvania convention that ratified the Constitution. In 1786 he published an educational project, with the arresting title "Thoughts Upon the Mode of Education Proper in a Republic." A few years later the American Philosophical Society offered a prize for "the best system of liberal education and literary instruction, adapted to the genius of the Government of the United States; comprehending also a plan for instituting and conducting public schools in this country, on principles of the most extensive utility." The prize was divided

---

[1] Wesley, E. B. *Proposed: The University of the United States.* Minneapolis: University of Minnesota Press, 1936. 83 p.

between Samuel Knox and Samuel H. Smith. Other thinkers of the age, including Noah Webster, presented to the public large projects for the education of youth in a manner appropriate to American society and government.

Early Educational Plans Were Wide
and Deep in Compass.

This is no place to describe these plans or to smooth away their inconsistencies, but a summary of them shows that American ideas on education are the treasures of high statesmanship—not merely the theories of school administrators and teachers.[1] Taking numerous plans of the early Republic collectively, we may say that they were amazingly broad and comprehensive. They projected institutions of learning extending from the primary schools to a national university in charge of research, general instruction, and training for the public service. They dealt with education in its widest terms, as adapted to the nature of American society and government, and as serving the progressive development of individuals and society—not the one or the other exclusively—but both as inseparable. These schemes were not confined to the practical arts and subjects of utility in the conduct of government. They did emphasize, it is true, the practical and political arts; but they went beyond any narrow utilitarianism. They included pure science, letters, and all the arts deemed necessary for a rich, secure, and enlightened civilization; and they recognized the truth that both government and economy rest upon wisdom, knowledge, and aspirations wider and deeper than the interests of immediate marketability.

---

[1] Hansen, Allen O. *Liberalism and American Education in the Eighteenth Century.* New York: Macmillan Co., 1926. 317 p.

The Role of Women in Civilization
Was Recognized.

In seeking to enrich the moral and intellectual resources
of society, some of the early educational planners gave
attention to the role of women as makers and bearers of
culture. They knew from impressive personal experience
the part that women had taken in the war for independence—for instance, in keeping economy running, in fur-
nishing war supplies, in sustaining and feeding the spirit of
independence in newspapers, pamphlets, and plays, and
in private councils. Leaders from General Washington
down the line had recognized their services and paid open
tribute to their part in the great drama.

It was no accident, then, that Noah Webster, perhaps
the most indefatigable among the educational leaders,
gave special consideration to the education of women. He
believed that their influence in shaping the underlying
ideals and policies of the nation was in many ways greater
than that of men. Mothers gave to youth firm impressions
of life's values and should be educated so that they would
set youth in the republican way of life. Taking this cultural influence into full account, Webster insisted that
the education of women "should therefore enable them to
implant in the tender mind such sentiments of virtue,
propriety, and dignity as are suited to the freedom of our
government." For this reason he insisted that their education should not be confined to subjects usually taught in
schools for girls, but should include science, history,
geography, contemporary affairs, and all that then passed
for the social studies. "In a system of education that
should embrace every part of the community," he urged,
"the female sex claims no inconsiderable part of our attention."

Freedom of Inquiry Was
Emphasized.

As befitted the temper of the age, early educational planners insisted upon unlimited freedom of inquiry and exposition in institutions of learning. They cast off *a priori* notions of tradition and brought to the bar of critical examination "all things under the sun"—the works of nature, institutions of Church and State, the forms and distribution of property, the relations of property to government, the processes of government, the driving forces of social life, the family and its historic role, the maxims of industry and commerce, and international affairs. And they did this with insight, a wealth of learning, and a firm grasp upon realities. For them, liberty of inquiry and exposition was not merely necessary to the working of popular institutions. It was indispensable to progress in every branch of human affairs. It was one of the noblest expressions of life among a free people. "What are the means of improving and establishing the Union of the States?" This was the question which Noah Webster encountered everywhere in his travels throughout the country in 1785. "Custom is the plague of wise men and the idol of fools!" he exclaimed. In this spirit, educational planners for the nation proposed to throw off denominational control of education, emphasized unhampered scientific research, and upheld the unfettered right of exposition, while cherishing a deep sense of social responsibility.

Education Was Deemed Indispensable
to Popular Government.

The men who had set up the new government after the Revolution were, as a matter of course, especially concerned with political education, with the preparation of the people for self-government. The processes of democracy to which they were committed, explicitly or implicitly, embraced five essential elements: the right of citizens to propose measures and policies, the right to discuss freely all proposed policies and measures, the right to decide issues at the polls, the obligation to accept decisions duly made without resort to force, and the right to appraise, criticize, and amend decisions so made. The preservation of these processes of democracy was assured in part, the founders believed, by laws and institutions guaranteeing freedom of the press, discussion, and decision, but they knew that paper guarantees were not enough. Knowledge and a moral sense were required to sustain democratic processes and to make them constructive, rather than destructive. "In proportion as the structure of government gives force to public opinion," wrote Washington in his Farewell Address, "it is essential that public opinion should be enlightened." How? "Promote, then, as an object of primary importance, institutions for the general diffusion of knowledge."

Education Was Considered in the Constitutional Convention of 1787.

In the convention that framed the Constitution, James Madison proposed that Congress be empowered "to establish a university," and Charles Pinckney urged a broader provision: "to establish seminaries for the promotion of literature and the arts and sciences." At a later time in the convention Madison and Pinckney joined in moving for the creation of a university. Upon their project Gouverneur Morris remarked: "It is not necessary. The exclusive power at the seat of government will reach the object." The motion was lost. No express provisions were made in the Constitution for the promotion of education, but leaders among the men who framed that document certainly believed that the power to perform this national service was positively implied. Even Jefferson, speaking later as a strict constructionist, declared that Congress could make appropriations of public lands for that purpose.

George Washington Advocated National Aids to Education.

That Washington regarded the fostering of education as an obligation of the Federal Government was made evident in his first annual address to Congress: "Nor am I less persuaded that you will agree with me in opinion that there is nothing which can better deserve your patronage than the promotion of science and literature. Knowledge is in every country the surest basis of public happiness. In one in which the measures of government receive their impressions so immediately from the sense of the community as in ours it is proportionably essential. To the security of a free constitution it contributes in various ways . . . Whether this desirable object will be best promoted by affording aids to seminaries of learning already established, by the institution of a national university, or by any other expedients will be well worthy of a place in the deliberations of the Legislature." In letters to his other colleagues, Washington also revealed his solicitude for education.

Washington Took a Broad View of Education.

And it was a broad interest. Although Washington, unlike Jefferson, had not enjoyed the privileges of a college education, and was a man of limited "book knowledge," he had a general and realistic view of education. Speaking of the proposed national university, he said: "I have greatly wished to see a plan adopted, by which the arts, science, and belles-lettres could be taught in their *fullest* extent, thereby embracing *all* the advantages of European tuition, with the means of acquiring the liberal knowledge, which is necessary to qualify our citizens for the exigencies of public as well as private life; and (which with me is a consideration of great magnitude) by assembling the youth from the different parts of this rising republic, contributing from their intercourse and interchange of information to the removal of prejudices, which might perhaps sometimes arise from local circumstances." So deeply impressed was he by the utility of such an institution that he left a part of his estate by will for the endowment of a university in the District of Columbia—a provision never acted upon by Congress.

Thomas Jefferson Made Education
a Primary Interest.

Although at odds with Washington on many points of policy and committed, while in the opposition, to a narrow construction of the Constitution, Thomas Jefferson was even more deeply and actively concerned with public education than the first President. As a biographer has truly said: "Jefferson was the first conspicuous advocate, in this country, of centralization in education, being a thorough believer in state aid to higher institutions of learning and free education in the common schools supported by local taxation. To him the schoolhouse was the fountain-head of happiness, prosperity, and good government, and education was 'a holy cause.'" A college graduate, a student of the classics, a leader in public affairs, interested in every branch of art, science, and letters, eager to make broad and deep the cultural foundations of democracy, Jefferson dedicated years of his life to the consideration and promotion of education in all its phases, from elementary instruction to advanced research in universities. He was, in many ways, the most highly cultivated man of his time, and, among the great directors of national affairs, he gave the most thought and personal attention to education.

His was no mere lip service. He sought to encompass education, to discover its possibilities, to give it an exalted and permanent position in public policy, and to make it enrich and serve the new society rising in America. It was characteristic of his concern that he omitted from the inscription which he prepared for his own tomb all mention of the high political offices he had held and included the fact that he was the founder of the University of Virginia.

Jefferson's Plan Included Wide Elementary Education.

Jefferson's plan of education for the state of Virginia embraced a scheme for elementary schools in every county, so placed that every householder would be within three miles of a school. On this base was to be erected district institutions of higher learning, so distributed that each student would be within a day's ride of a college. Crowning the structure was a university of the highest type dedicated to the freedom of the mind and unlimited research for truth. That sons of the poor might not be denied the privileges of education, Jefferson proposed that "the best genius" of each elementary school, if unable to pay his way, should be sent to the secondary school at public expense, and that the ablest in each secondary institution be maintained at the university free of cost. Thus the elements of learning were to be made available to all, and for the ablest boys, even those without financial resources, the pathway to the university was to be opened. Although the plan was never enacted into law, Jefferson saw clearly that the nation needed talent in public and private affairs, and education was to enable talent to flower.

Jefferson's Educational Objectives for Lower Schools Were Individual and Social.

In no single place did Jefferson summarize his philosophy of education, but the following passage from his writings indicates the nature of his thought respecting the ends to be attained:

"(1) To give to every citizen the information he needs for the transaction of his own business;

"(2) To enable him to calculate for himself, and to express and preserve his ideas, his contracts, and accounts, in writing;

"(3) To improve, by reading, his morals and faculties;

"(4) To understand his duties to his neighbors and country, and to discharge with competence the functions confided to him by either;

"(5) To know his rights; to exercise with order and justice those he retains; to choose with discretion the fiduciary of those he delegates; and to notice their conduct with diligence, with candor and judgment;

"(6) And, in general, to observe with intelligence and faithfulness all the social relations under which he shall be placed."

For His University Jefferson Proclaimed
Untrammelled Liberty of Inquiry.

As the motto for his University of Virginia, Jefferson chose the ancient saying: "And ye shall know the truth, and the truth shall make you free." In that spirit he stipulated complete freedom of inquiry and exposition for the professors, self-government for the faculty, and an honor system for the students. "I have sworn upon the altar of God," he exclaimed, "eternal hostility against every form of tyranny over the mind of man."

In His University Curriculum Jefferson Emphasized
the Social and Natural Sciences.

In laying out a program of university work, Jefferson placed emphasis on the social and natural sciences in a manner so comprehensive that his project may be still studied with advantage, and employed as a guide for educational thought. Its great purposes may be summarized in the language of a special student of Jeffersonian policies:

"(1) To form the statesmen, legislators, and judges, on whom public prosperity and individual happiness depend;

"(2) To expound the principles and structure of government, the laws which regulate the intercourse of nations, those formed municipally for our own government, and a sound spirit of legislation;

"(3) To harmonize and promote the interests of agriculture, manufactures, and commerce, and by well-informed views of political economy to give a free scope to the public industry;

"(4) To develop the reasoning faculties of our youth, enlarge their minds, cultivate their morals, and instill in them the precepts of virtue and order; and

"(5) To enlighten them with mathematical and physical sciences, which advance the arts, and administer to the health, the subsistence, and comforts of human life."

To Jefferson nothing human was alien; neither the thought of Virgil, nor the invention of a threshing machine. To preserve, advance, and disseminate knowledge in the improvement of individual well-being and social relations was, for Jefferson, a passion that endured to his last days.

Jefferson Regarded Education as a Combined National and State Interest

Despite his immediate concern with education in Virginia, Jefferson was also engrossed in education as a national interest. In his message of December 2, 1806, he suggested the appropriation of public funds "to the great purposes of the public education, roads, rivers, canals, and such other objects of public improvement as it may be thought proper to add to the constitutional enumeration of Federal powers." He was prepared to amend the Constitution, if necessary to promote education and economic welfare, but he recognized the fact that Congress already had some authority over these matters, including the power to dedicate public lands to "a national establishment of education." Again, in 1808, in his last message, Jefferson called upon Congress to consider the same theme. Thus even amid the turmoil of the Napoleonic wars, which violently disturbed the politics and economy of the United States, the President continued to urge upon Congress and the country an interest that lay close to his heart.

John Quincy Adams Emulated the
Example of Washington.

With the administration of John Quincy Adams, "the heroic period of the Revolution" drew to a close. In a strict sense Adams did not belong to it, but as a boy he had gone to Europe and assumed the duties of secretary to his father on a mission for the Republic then battling for existence. He was brought up in the Washington tradition and derived conceptions of policy from that source. Having started life as a Federalist and having transferred his allegiance to the Jeffersonian party, Adams found it possible to combine, in his thought, elements from the two systems of statesmanship. Unlike James Monroe, his immediate predecessor, Adams had no doubts about the constitutionality of the broad views entertained by Washington. With the exception of Jefferson, no President had been more deeply interested in natural science and its beneficent applications than John Quincy Adams. If he could have had his way, the nation's great endowment in natural resources would have been conserved and dedicated to internal improvements, the advancement of science, and the promotion of education. It was with extreme bitterness that he spoke of the "rapacity" with which politicians "fly at the public lands," engage in "pillage," and act as "enormous speculators and landjobbers."

Adams Urged Congress To Promote Science,
Education, and the Arts.

Seeking to resist the pressure for the dissipation of the national resources, Adams urged upon Congress a broader social policy. "The great object of the institution of civil

[25]

government," he said in his first annual message, "is the improvement of the condition of those who are parties to the social compact, and no government, in whatever form constituted, can accomplish the lawful ends of its institution but in proportion as it improves the condition of those over whom it is established. Roads and canals, by multiplying and facilitating the communications and intercourse between distant regions and multitudes of men, are among the most important means of improvement. But moral, political, intellectual improvement are duties assigned by the Author of Our Existence to social no less than to individual man. For the fulfilment of those duties governments are invested with power, and to the attainment of the end—the progressive improvement of the condition of the governed—the exercise of delegated powers is a duty as sacred and indispensable as the usurpation of powers not granted is criminal and odious. Among the first, perhaps the very first, instrument for the improvement of the condition of men is knowledge, and to the acquisition of much of the knowledge adapted to the wants, the comforts, and enjoyments of human life public institutions and seminaries of learning are essential."

After laying down this controlling principle, Adams then urged the promotion of "scientific research and inquiry" in "geographical and astronomical science," the exploration of national territories and waters, the erection of an astronomical observatory "connected with the establishment of an university, or separate from it," the patronage of studies in the science of weights and measures, and the revision of the patent laws. Summarizing the powers of Congress, Adams indicated that they could be brought into action "by laws promoting the improvement of agriculture, commerce, and manufactures, the cultivation and encouragement of the mechanic and of the elegant arts, the advancement of literature, and the progress of the sciences, ornamental and profound."

If the language of these reflections and recommendations is somewhat stilted, there is no doubt respecting its thought and import. Adams had in mind a conception of the nation as a civilization and the use of its material, intellectual, and moral resources, under public auspices, in "the progressive improvement of the condition of the governed." The powers of the Federal Government he deemed ample for this purpose and refusal to use them, he thought, "would be treachery to the most sacred of trusts." "The spirit of improvement," he exclaimed, "is abroad upon the earth." Should the Federal Government fall behind state governments in "holding up the torch of human improvement to eyes that seek the light?"

But the Times Were Not Favorable for the Promotion of Plans for Education.

Admirable and promising as were many of these plans for education, the times were not propitious for bringing them to fruition. The great social and economic forces which were to call them into being some forty or fifty years after the adoption of the Constitution had not yet appeared. The population of America consisted of between three and four million persons, thinly scattered over a wide area. Rural civilization predominated. As late as 1820 less than five percent of the total population lived in the thirteen cities of 8,000 or over. Slow, crude means of transportation and communication resulted in isolation for most of the people. Collective action was extremely difficult. Moreover, the war for independence had exhausted the resources of the government and had left a war debt which threatened to keep them depleted over a period of years. The people were engrossed with political matters.

As a consequence of these adverse conditions, education declined to its lowest point since schools were founded by the colonists. The close of the period found local authority strongly entrenched in the administration of education. There was as yet no sign of that integration of small local schools into state school systems which came within the next fifty years. Although during the early national period the Federal Government began the policy of making land grants which forecast universal education, such grants are more accurately interpreted as a stimulus to the colonization of new territory than as a national policy whose primary purpose was to promote education. In general the National Government followed the policy of leaving the provision and administration of education to the states and local communities. Educational as well as national consciousness was yet to awaken, and it was not until some years after the second war with England that plans for popular education began to receive serious consideration; then, state plans, not national plans, were adopted as the schools passed from an administration predominantly local to an administration and control originating with the state.

Though Temporarily Rejected, the Educational Ideals of the Founders Remain Basic for Contemporary Thought.

It so happened, then, that the founders of the Republic did not live to see their ideals realized in the establishment of public institutions for education. For this outcome lack of popular interest, the opposition of private schools, and poverty of financial resources were partly responsible. Doubtless even more influential was the popular revolt against the broad conceptions of federal policy which they cherished. With the triumph of Andrew Jackson in 1828

[28]

the principles of the Federalist party, with which Washington was associated in spirit, and the principles of the Republican party, which Jefferson led, were repudiated in a surge of democracy that was suspicious of all government and soon fell under the dominance of the particularism known as states' rights. Events thus provided a new setting of ideas and interests for the period in which institutions of popular education were actually created and for educational thought itself. In other words, the age of concentration that marked the foundation of the Republic was followed by an age of diffusion, in which the security and perpetuity of the nation were largely taken for granted, despite the shadows of civil dissension. Yet, while the work of establishing institutions of public education fell principally to the states and communities, the Union organized by the founders was continued and furnished the institutional frame in which economy was being nationalized even while particularism seemed triumphant.

III.

Democracy and Individualism Provided the Context for Public Education.

Taken as a whole the age which opened with the advent of Jackson was characterized by an intense reaction against the cultural outlook of Washington, Madison, Jefferson, and John Quincy Adams. This reaction culminated in a conception that America was not a nation at all, but an aggregation of sovereign states, any one of which could legally withdraw from the Union at its pleasure. Associated with it, as a matter of course, was the repudiation of the idea that the Government of the United States should be employed in promoting agriculture, manufactures, commerce, and internal improvements, the advancement of science, literature, and the arts, and the development of education. As a corollary, stress was laid on individual liberty in economy, individual equality in democracy, and individual rights against society. This reaction, by its very nature, meant a dispersion of energies, not a concentration such as had carried through the Revolution against Great Britain, the establishment of the Constitution, and the formulation of economic and social policies on a national scale. It was on this tide in American affairs that were floated the philosophy and practice of public education which were to become dominant in later years.

The Industrial Revolution Made Rapid Headway.

In matters of economy, the second period of American history was marked by tendencies that differentiated it from the age of the founders. These may be swiftly summarized: the rapid rise of machine industries, driving handicrafts and small shops to the wall; the growth of corporations in industry, commerce, and finance, bringing new forms of property ownership; the spread of steam transportation in commerce; the swift upswing of commercial and industrial cities, raising the problem of urban aggregations that had long vexed the Old World; periodical crises in economy such as occurred in 1837, 1846, 1857, and 1873, making acute the uncertainties and insecurities of life; the opening wide of national gates to poverty-stricken immigrants from the Old World; the development of a huge body of industrial workers, with labor organizations, conflicts, and strikes disturbing to social peace; the transformation of slavery from the domestic system of the old days into the capitalistic cotton planting system and finally its destruction in a civil war; the opening of the Near and Far West by farm settlements, with their forms and practices of agrarian democracy; the drive of cotton planting into the Southwest and the extension of the national domain to the Pacific Coast; the alienation of the nation's immense endowment in land and other natural resources into private property, to be exploited by private initiative for private profit without control by the National Government. Thus the relatively compact nation of the seaboard was expanded from ocean to ocean, and its economy—industrial and agricultural—revolutionized by events.

*These New Forces Made for Integration
in American Education.*

While the dominant political tendency of this period was toward the surrender of authority to the states, social and economic forces far more powerful and permanent in

American life were running against this centrifugal movement. In many of the most important phases of local, state, and national affairs, coordinating and integrating influences were rapidly consolidating the people and were making for unity in customs, habits, and interests which were in strong contrast to the highly individualized life of the past. The growth of cities, improvement in transportation and communication, the development of corporate action by both industry and labor and many other evidences of the striking tendency toward group life ended forever the long period of isolation and made possible effective group action. The collective influence of these mighty forces created a solidarity in American life not to be nullified by any contradictory philosophy, by whatever powerful hands wielded.

The schools were among those institutions and agencies which were affected by the unifying forces of this period. Within a relatively short time, scattered district schools were being welded into state school systems under the leadership of such men as Carter, Mann, and Barnard. In the cities, schools founded by charity and philanthropy were replaced by schools supported and administered by the civil unit and with the stigma of pauperism lifted from those who attended them. Even the frontier, injecting as it did powerful disintegrating influences into national political life, demanded state school systems to provide equality of educational opportunity for its people. At the beginning of the Jacksonian period education for the masses of the people was little more than a hazy ideal of theorists and reformers; by the middle of the century it became an actuality for millions of the people.

Equalitarian Democracy
Made Swift Gains.

In the sphere of government, the immediate reaction against the "aristocratic" features of the early Republic was intense. The doctrine of equality had been proclaimed by the Declaration of Independence; now it was applied by the extension of the suffrage to white males without distinctions of property in law. Appealing to the logic of the theory, women held their first national suffrage convention in 1848 and launched a campaign for universal suffrage. Observing the trend everywhere in Western civilization, Thomas Carlyle exclaimed: "Universal democracy, whatever we may think of it, has declared itself as an inevitable fact of the days in which we live; and he who has any chance to instruct, or lead, in his day, must begin by admitting that."

With the extension of the suffrage came popular election of presidential electors, the rise of the party nominating conventions, and the wresting of government from the old "aristocracy of wealth and talents." For a more or less permanent public service were substituted rotation in office, short terms, and the spoils system. "The duties of any public office," declared Andrew Jackson, "are so simple or admit of being made so simple that any man can in a short time become master of them." Henceforward, for many years, men who had dwelt in log cabins or humble homes were to occupy the White House so long possessed by gentlemen in powdered wigs and knee breeches.

The Functions of the Federal Government
Were Curtailed.

Respecting federal economic policies, the upheaval during the opening years of the second period was likewise thoroughgoing. The national bank was destroyed; for it were substituted state banks, with their "wild cat" tendencies. Internal improvements were found to be unconstitutional and this phase of federal activity was slowed down. National aids to commerce and shipping were either curtailed or abandoned. In its platform of 1844 the Democratic party set forth the political science of the membership. It declared that all grants of power in the Constitution "ought to be strictly construed . . . and it is inexpedient and dangerous to exercise doubtful constitutional powers." It proclaimed "an equality of rights and privileges." The Federal Government should not "foster one branch of industry to the detriment of another." This Government has no power to charter a United States Bank; such an institution is "dangerous to our republican institutions and the liberties of the people." To crown the system of Federal retrenchment, the Democratic party added a resolution in 1856 that the people of the United States should declare themselves in favor of "progressive free trade throughout the world."

The Triumph of the Republican Party in 1865
Continued the Cultural Tradition of
Jacksonian Democracy.

Although the triumph of the second Republican party and the preservation of the Union in the civil conflict brought a reversal of these policies in many respects, they did not effect a return to the system of the early Republic. That party took for its name the title of Jefferson's party; and its first great leader, Abraham Lincoln, derived ideas and inspiration from the teachings of Jefferson. But America did not recover 1789 in the victory of 1865. Popular suffrage remained and was widened; the political practices of democracy, including the spoils system, were continued; the ideal of universal equality was strengthened by the abolition of chattel slavery.

While renewing the patronage of industry, commerce, and agriculture by Federal action, national leadership continued the policy of transforming national resources into private property—with swiftness and prodigality. It deplored all Federal intervention with economy, save that designed to promote active interests. At the same time, the Fourteenth Amendment to the Constitution, as interpreted by the Supreme Court, restricted social legislation in the states by curtailing their police power. If, as sometimes contended, leadership in the second half of the nineteenth century combined the Federalism of Washington with the Democracy of Jefferson, it certainly did not display the whole cultural outlook of these national statesmen; nor did it accord to education the role in civilization accepted by Washington, Jefferson, and John Quincy Adams.

No National Statesman Assumed
Leadership in Education.

After the close of John Quincy Adams' administration no great leader in national affairs looked all around education, plumbed its depths, considered its relation to the nation, and, like Washington, Jefferson, and John Quincy Adams, staked his reputation upon urging its promotion in every department—from elementary instruction to the highest inquiry and research. General tributes were paid to education by national statesmen, aspects of it were touched upon, and money was voted for its support. But exploration of its relation to government, economy, and civilization was neglected by the directors of Federal affairs after that time. Nor did leaders of great private

[36]

affairs dedicate high talents and powers of mind to this subject. They too offered praise to education and generously poured out millions for private endowments. Occasionally they lauded, if pleased; and protested if displeased; but where in their writings, addresses, and testaments did they display anything like Washington's or Jefferson's encompassing and penetrating grasp of the thought, activities, and expositions which they endowed?

In keeping with the ascendant conceptions of the age, leadership in educational advocacy, surrendered by Presidents and national statesmen, was carried forward by private citizens, local statesmen, and especially professional educators. The break with the past was not absolute, of course; but the emphasis was different and other conceptions of society, government, and public policy prevailed generally. The age was also marked for a time by preoccupation with the civil conflict, and then with the exploitation of the continental domain, under different auspices and yet under Jacksonian theories of public policy, especially with respect to the disposition of natural resources, the obligations of government, and the nature of its social responsibilities.

It is true that Congress passed in 1862 the Morrill Act, granting land for the establishment of colleges by the states, and later subsidized agricultural experiment stations; that the Department of Education, soon reduced to the status of a Bureau, was set up in 1867; and that President Ulysses S. Grant renewed the old recommendation of a national university in his message of 1873. Still these events, however important in themselves, were incidents, not primary concerns, in national politics. Education continued to be entrusted to local inspiration, leadership, and control.

The Idea of Political and Economic Individualism
Was Accepted as an Automatic Guarantee
of Progress and Order.

In turning from the features of economy and politics to the general ideas uppermost in this period, we encounter complexities more difficult to summarize. Yet in the long perspective we can discern certain dominant ideas amid the tumult and conflict. Perhaps first among them must be placed the idea of complete equality for all individuals in government, economy, and cultural opportunity. With a growing insistence this idea rang through the thought of the age. Coupled with it was a conception of social policy deemed essential to the realization of equality in opportunity. That conception called for "giving everybody a chance" to acquire fame and fortune, for the transformation of the national domain into private property, and for emphasis on individual initiative and liberty in the use of property—with government or collective action reduced to the minimum. It embraced what John R. Commons calls the "mechanical principles of individualism, selfishness, division of labor, exchange of commodities, equality, fluidity, liberty, and that divine providence which led individuals to benefit each other without intending to do so." That the new social policy was a driving influence in the extraordinary development of the material resources of the nation can scarcely be controverted. That it appeared to be then the final word in statescraft is not surprising to students of intellectual history.

The ruling conception of the time, ascribed with some disregard for truth to Thomas Jefferson, was succinctly and appropriately stated in 1860 by James Parton, the biographer of Andrew Jackson. According to the new creed: "the office of government is solely to maintain justice between man and man, and between the nation and other nations. It should have nothing to do with carrying letters, supporting schools, digging canals, constructing railroads, or establishing scientific institutions. Its business is simply to suppress villains, foreign and domestic. The people are to be left absolutely free to work out their welfare in their own way. . . . Paternal government establishes and supports schools; Jeffersonian government ordains (or should) that no ignoramus shall vote, and sees to it (or should) that no parent, guardian, or master *defrauds* a child, ward, or apprentice of the means of acquiring knowledge. . . . This theory of government, incompletely set forth in the writings of Mr. Jefferson, has been recently elaborated with singular lucidity and power by an English author, Mr. Herbert Spencer, whose work on 'Social Statics' Mr. Jefferson ought to have lived long enough to read, such keen delight would he have had in seeing his cherished opinion stated with the clearness of light, and demonstrated as Euclid demonstrates propositions in geometry." This is the system which Carlyle characterized as anarchy plus the police constable. That it was often violated in practice by Jacksonian democracy, and later by other national measures, is evident in the records of history; but it was long a prominent characteristic of American thought and life.

Darwinism Fortified the Idea of Individual Struggle for Existence.

Powerfully affecting the thought of the age was the idea of natural science, theoretical and applied. It was, in brief, the idea that the material world, and, to some extent at least, human affairs, are governed by immutable laws which can be revealed by research and employed to effect

[39]

human purposes. Among the many findings reported in the name of science in this period was one which fortified the prevailing conception of social policy, namely, the theory of the struggle for existence, associated with Darwinism. Although one-sided in its emphasis and oblivious to other factors in the evolution of the species, such as mutual aid, it was added to the formulas of politics and economics and seemed to lend the sanction of all nature to a tooth and claw struggle of individuals for wealth and position. In the hands of Herbert Spencer, and as popularized in the United States by John Fiske, it lent intellectual, if not moral, support to dominant conceptions of economy, government, and social policy in general.

Yet the Evils of Poverty Shadow the March of Progress.

Nevertheless, it could not be said that contentment with the course of affairs in the United States during these long years was universal. Far from it. Coupled all along with praise for the acts of the times were dissatisfactions and aspirations coming under the broad head of social reform and manifesting themselves in third parties and rifts in the major parties. Even before the advent of Jacksonian democracy, and certainly after the financial crash of 1837, observers of American society called attention, with increasing reiteration, not only to slavery in the South but to poverty and degradation in the industrial regions of the North. It was not merely in the writings of agitators deemed radical, such as Josiah Warren, Frances Wright, and Wendell Phillips, that this concern with distress and poverty appeared. Great leaders of American thought— for example, Emerson, Horace Greeley, Charles A. Dana, and James Russell Lowell—were deeply moved by the human degradation that accompanied "the march of progress."

As remedies for the evils discovered, numerous panaceas were offered to the public. In the early days of the Jacksonian epoch, the project of utopian socialism, or cooperative colonies, was powerfully sponsored by leading personalities, among them Horace Greeley. When repeated failures damped their ardors and hopes, the reformers offered two other methods of coping with poverty and degradation, as ways of escape and as promises of security and liberty. One of them was the plan of the agrarians for giving away the public domain as free homesteads to settlers. This, it was argued, would enable the distressed to find liberty and a living on the land and permit those who remained behind to raise their wages by threats of wholesale emigration to the West. Into this movement for land reform, utopian socialists and labor leaders finally threw great energies and won from Congress the Homestead Act of 1862. The other grand project for eliminating the poverty and wretchedness that haunted American society was public education.

IV.

Educational Philosophy Was Adapted to the Spirit of the Age.

Such were relevant circumstances in which public education, largely a hope in the early days of the Republic, took on its philosophy and practice, and flowered into a state system, with regional connections and outlook. Such was the general context of ideas and interests in which Horace Mann, Henry Barnard, Mary Lyon, Emma Willard, Calvin Wiley, J. L. M. Curry, William T. Harris, and a veritable host of American citizens formulated the theory and built up the institutions of public education in the states, with achievements to their credit little short of the seven wonders of the world. It was not in a shadowy realm of abstractions that they wrought. As the hand is subdued to the dye in which it works, so their minds and aspirations were conditioned by the essential concerns of the age in which their lot was cast.

That the dominant ideas and interests of the time entered into the formulation of the conceptions and objectives of education is shown by Curti.[1] Among these conceptions and objectives a few stand out impressively. An analysis and classification of them are necessary to a comprehension of the educational system which the early leaders created and bequeathed to posterity—the system in which our generation has worked. Professor Curti does not say that a single pattern of thought existed in identical form in the minds of all leaders who took part in founding and developing public schools. Some leaders em-

---

[1] Curti, Merle. *The Social Ideas of American Educators.* New York: Charles Scribner's Sons, 1935. 613 p.

phasized one aspect; others laid their main stress elsewhere. But when their patterns of thought are laid on top of one another, certain centers of interest correspond, despite differences and shadings.

Education Was Conceived as an Aid in
Sustaining Democratic Government.

Without making a hazardous attempt to arrange them in order of historical importance, we may begin with the emphasis on public education as a promise for the fulfilment of the democratic ideal, as an instrument for making democratic government adequate to the exigencies of society, and as a corrective for the "evils" of the wider democracy brought about by the extension of the suffrage in Jacksonian days. At last the decision on momentous questions that had long vexed mankind was entrusted to masses of the people, and Horace Mann offered public education as the supreme hope for wise and just decisions. "The rack, the faggot, and the dungeon," he said, had failed to decide them; "the blood of all the martyrs" had failed; "the power of kings aided by the wealth of nations" had failed. If these issues were ever to be correctly settled, Mann thought, "it must be by each party's laying aside its exclusiveness, its pride, its infallibility, its contempt, and, by the union of all in some noble plan, to give to another generation fitter attainments, greater capacities, and that without which all other means are worthless— minds free from prejudice, and yearning after truth."

Yet there were dangers in the popular experiment. Masses of propertyless white men were given the vote and the right to hold office. This was a break with history, with the conceptions and practices of the men who founded the American Republic. In a sense it was, as contended by the opponents at the time, revolutionary in nature and import. In opposing a system of complete political equality, Daniel Webster, as a member of the Massachusetts constitutional convention of 1820, warned his auditors that political equality and economic inequality were incompatible; that political equality would bring assaults on private property, or compel "the holders of estates" to limit the right of suffrage. It was with some such warnings in mind that Horace Mann, successor of John Quincy Adams in the House of Representatives, "turned to universal education as the best insurance against mobocracy, confiscatory legislation, threats to judicial supremacy, and the spoils system which Jacksonism held so dear." Public education, it was repeatedly argued, would develop good citizens, calm popular distempers, and make the success of democracy possible.

The Assimilation of Aliens Was Made
a Function of Education.

A second function assigned to public education by the leaders was the assimilation of the aliens who poured into the country, as growing industries and the development of agriculture opened the way for them. The thin stream of early republican days became a flood at the middle of the nineteenth century, and a torrent at the close. Men, women, and children of many races, usually poverty-stricken, uneducated, speaking a babel of tongues, imbued with other traditions, streamed into the United States by the millions. Owners of mines, factories, and industries welcomed them; land speculators greeted them with effusion. Many of the immigrants crowded into urban areas; ethnic groups formed cities of their own within cities, and preserved a separatism on which politicians and demagogues played in their struggle for power. As historians were fond of pointing out, the invasions which disrupted the Roman Empire were relatively trivial in point of numbers. The perils were evident, and to public education was assigned the herculean task of teaching immigrants the English language, preparing them for crafts and callings in the United States, and instructing them in respect of the spirit and practices of American institutions. The fact that some European authorities were deliberately emptying their poorhouses on our shores gave to this argument for education a point which could scarcely be missed.

Education Was Regarded as an Aid in Assuring Equality of Preparation for Economic Opportunity.

Within the policy set for government and economy, the public schools were also to prepare boys and girls for making the most of their opportunities, for rising in the world to positions of wealth and influence. American democracy had proclaimed equality, had asserted the right of every individual to advance as far as his talents could carry him, and had thrown open the public domain to swift and unrestricted exploitation. An apparently obvious corollary of this policy was the equalization of opportunities for all to acquire the knowledge and training required for the race in which victory went to talents, as distinguished from the privileges of birth. On this aspect of public education, organized labor laid heavy emphasis, early and late. It demanded public support for education, to remove the stigma of pauperism which marked many of the charity schools. It opposed mere manual training, as designed to fix class lines, and insisted upon a system of education that would provide "ladders" to the highest and most lucrative places in the country.

[46]

If America was to be regarded as "the land of opportunity," if opportunities were to be "equal," then education must provide "the equal start."

The Undeveloped Resources of the Nation Seemed
To Offer Endless Economic Opportunity.

The logic of the plan seemed overwhelming. Circumstances seemed propitious for its application. American industries were young and no one could set limits to their expansion. American agriculture had a continental domain to conquer. Debaters in Congress pointed out as late as 1852 that, in the preceding sixty years, only 100,-000,000 acres of the public land had been sold, and that 1,400,000,000 remained in the hands of the National Government. From such figures the conclusion was drawn that it would take from 400 to 900 years, at the existing rate of sale, to reach the end. With such a pleasing economic prospect spread out before them, the sponsors of public education could with good reason proclaim opportunity; committed to the principle of equality for all, they could plead for equal educational facilities.

Education Set to Work within the
Frame of a Noble Dream.

By inculcating loyalty to the democratic order, by the training of citizens, by the assimilation of aliens, and by the equalization of educational opportunities, founders of the public schools hoped to realize in America a noble social dream with liberty, justice, and welfare for all. In this society careers were to be open to everybody, talents were to be efficiently applied in the exploitation of the national endowment and the production of wealth, and the blessings of civilization were to be shared by all. If the initiative of individuals could be given liberty, if they could be equipped with knowledge of the practical arts, then there would be prosperity and security for American society in the years to come. So thought Horace Mann. Oppressed by the economic misery which he saw about him, Mann was inspired to passionate labor in behalf of education as a hope for an escape from poverty. Henry Barnard and Catherine Beecher were no less haunted by the spectre; and they likewise looked to public education as the means of laying it forever.

Public Education Forged Ahead.

Driven by the dynamic of these powerful considerations, public education made headway against popular indifference and privileged hostility, from small beginnings to magnificence of resources and vastness of plant. Heirs and followers of this tradition accepted its assumptions, worked within its boundaries, devised new methods for achieving the original purposes, and appeared to expect an endless expansion.

There were doubters, to be sure. Horace Greeley, the inveterate reformer, bluntly asked: "To the child daily sent out from a rickety hovel or miserable garret to wrestle with Poverty and Misery for such knowledge as the teacher can impart, what true idea or purpose of Education is possible?" But even Greeley came to regard free homesteads as the escape from poverty, and in the end conceded the point of the educators. By this combination America could be made the land of opportunity; through equal education the children of landless farmers, poverty-stricken immigrants, and city slum dwellers might find their way outward, if not upward, into security, perhaps affluence.

This Long Period Presents Three Phases in the
Development of Public Education.

Early political leaders saw in education a pledge of
national unity, a support for popular government, an
instrument of intellectual emancipation, a servant of the
practical arts, and a guarantee that talents would be supplied for public and private affairs. In the middle period,
when public education was actually established, the human-
itarians sought to make education democratic and universal, a bulwark against the evils and excesses of popular
tumults in government, an agency for the assimilation of
aliens, and an equalizer in preparation for taking advantage
of the opportunities presented by American life and
economy. Thereafter, while the American continental
domain was being developed and exploited, while economic
opportunities were unfolding rapidly, while American
society seemed to be advancing steadily, without any
profound disturbances, professional leadership made the
schools more effective agencies of education—through
research, studies of individual differences, the perfection
of methods, the extension of teacher training, and the
improvement of administration.

Events Marched While Educational Leadership
Concentrated on Immediate Obligations.

As the nineteeth century turned into the twentieth,
many forces conspired to concentrate the energies of educational leadership on the immediate tasks at hand. The
mere burden of caring for millions of children was itself
enormous. The scientific spirit fostered by learning en-
couraged specialization—the investigation of the minute
in the search for more exact truth. The weight of admin-

istrative and classroom routine was oppressive, curtailing the time and strength available for the consideration of education as a function of the highest intelligence and the most imperative moral power. Like law, medicine, and other professions, education showed the perhaps inevitable tendency to turn in upon itself and to become specialized, technical, and separated more or less from the pulsing currents of American life. Nevertheless, events continued to march outside the confines of the administrative office, the schoolroom, and the professional gathering. The social order in which education worked was changed under the impacts of world-wide shocks. The loosely knit society, of 1850 let us say, was transformed into the highly integrated and interdependent society of 1937 which laid on professional leadership the task of making education socially significant and efficient. New times called for the application of the Socratic elenchus to ruling principles, accepted maxims, and standardized performances.

V.

New Interests and Ideas Demand Educational Readjustments.

The middle period of American history, with its dominant interests and ideas, has closed. And what have been the outcomes of the equalitarian democracy adopted in that period, the political and economic policies pursued, the practices for the disposition of natural resources followed, the educational philosophy formulated? With the present in front of us, and the future on the horizon, this is one of the supreme questions for educational leadership. If, as we may believe, the present and future are rooted in the developments of the past, if the early leaders were right in relating educational philosophy to the conditions and prospects of society, then we too must face this question, and answer it out of such knowledge as we can command. Again summaries are necessary.

Political Democracy Remains.

Thus far the popular institutions of government founded in the eighteenth century, and widened into the democracy of Jackson and Lincoln, have survived. Indeed they have been extended, by the emancipation of slaves, the partial enfranchisement of Negroes, and the addition of woman suffrage. Moreover, other institutions of democracy, such as initiative, referendum, recall, and direct primary, have been grafted on the original stock. With popular government breaking down in Europe and challenged everywhere in the name of authority and force, the development of democracy has continued unabated in America.

The Functions of Political Government Have Multiplied.

But the few and simple functions of government prevailing in the early period—the functions of "the police state"—have been supplemented by functions bewildering in variety—social services undreamt of, save by a few, at the middle of the nineteeth century. A mere description of them fills volumes.[1] So, with the growth of political democracy, the obligations of popular government underwent a revolution.

Over Free Land Sweeps Tenancy.

What became, however, of the "free land" and "unlimited resources" which were to furnish opportunities for security and a livelihood—for 400 or 900 years? By 1890, that fictitious year which marked "the closing of the frontier," practically all the good arable land available to homesteaders had been granted away, and the rest of the free land open to settlement was of low quality. By that fateful year "only 372,659 homestead entries had been perfected, granting 48,225,736 acres to supposed settlers—an area less than that of the state of Nebraska and equal only to three and one-half per cent of the total territory west of the Mississippi River. By that date more than four times as much land had been given to the railroad compa-

---

[1] President's Research Committee, Wesley C. Mitchell, chairman. *Recent Social Trends in the United States.* New York: McGraw-Hill Book Co., 1933. 2 vols. ¶Wooddy, Carroll H. *Growth of the Federal Government, 1915-1932.* New York: McGraw-Hill Book Co., 1934. 577 p.

nies." Between 1870 and 1890, "as the population increased 63½ per cent, manufacturing labor more than doubled in number while the total engaged in agriculture grew by only 45 per cent." Surveying the state of things at the end of that period, "the Industrial Commission accounted for 8,395,634 persons engaged in agriculture in 1890, of whom 3,004,061 were hired laborers. In addition there were no less than 1,500,000 tenant workmen. This leaves less than 4,000,000 persons tilling land of their own, including all the mortgaged farms. Only three-eighths of the families of the United States were cultivating the soil 'as owners, tenants, or laborers,' and the ratio was declining constantly. Over half of these were on an economic basis scarcely if any better than that of the city laborer."[1] The fortunes of farmers, tenants, share croppers, field laborers, and migratory agricultural laborers after 1890 need no recapitulation here. The cumulative effects are recorded in the census returns in pitiless figures, revealing cultural implications that reach the very depths of American life. School graduates by the millions can no longer look forward to free homesteads on which to apply their talents and energies.

*The Call for Conservation Checks the Rush
of Unrestrained Exploitation.*

Within fifty years after they were made, prophecies of opportunities in agriculture for 400 or 900 years were belied by events. There was no more free arable land of real quality. Nearly all of the best forest, mineral, and grazing land had been alienated for exploitation by private enterprise. By that time the Government of the United States

[1] Shannon, F. A. "The Homestead Act and the Labor Surplus," *American Historical Review* 41:637-51; July, 1936.

was turning its back upon its historic policies, as indicated by the enactment of 1891 which provided for the creation of forest reserves on the remaining public domain. Now, in our day, the Government has been called upon by a half-frantic people to irrigate deserts, to protect whole regions against the floods that descend from denuded hills, to reforest slashed and ruined acres by the million, to restore to grass millions of acres that never should have been given to the plough, to do battle with dust storms, and to resettle beaten and destitute farming families that sought opportunity in the West. *Each* farmer, as Adam Smith might say, knew best what to do with his land; but he could not forecast distant results after *all* farmers had long followed their immediate interests—had drained swamps, cut down trees, and lowered water levels for regions vast in expanse; nor did he know the effect of his own output in the market on which his prices and standard of life depended. After a comprehensive survey of the tendency of things in the use of our natural resources, the engineers of the National Resources Board set forth in cold realism, in 1935, the ruinous prospects of land and water resources, unless historic practices are discontinued.

Corporate Ownership Overshadows
Individual Ownership in Industry.

During the long period in which educational philosophy and the public schools were taking form and developing, profound changes were occurring in industrial organization and procedure—in that world of economic opportunities for which the schools were training millions of pupils annually. In the production of staple commodities, the small local plant individually or corporately owned, and operated by a small number of employees, gave way to the gigantic plant or system of plants corporately owned and employing thousands of workers. By 1930 corporations owned and controlled approximately 78 per cent of American business wealth, and two hundred of the largest corporations owned and controlled about 38 per cent of all business wealth. In substance this corporate development made a revolution in the types of industrial opportunities and practices prevailing when public education was established. It marked a large-scale transfer of individual ownership from real property to paper, the creation of heavy fiduciary obligations, a thoroughgoing alteration in the working relations of employers and employees, and the imposition of new restraints on possibilities of rising into the ownership and management of real property.

Local Economies Are Tied into National Economy.

Accompanying this growth of corporate ownership and management was a specialization of industry and agriculture by commodities, regions, and groups. For diversified local factories that supplied nearly all community wants were substituted specialized industries relying upon national and international markets for survival and prosperity. For the self-sufficing homestead was substituted the one-crop system—the dairy farm, the wheat farm, the cattle ranch, or the fruit and vegetable farm. Inevitably there was a corresponding growth of interstate commerce and interdependence among regions, industries, and occupations. Associated with this growth came an integration of specialized industries through industrial corporations and super-corporations, investment concerns, banking institutions, and holding companies—in spite of the anti-trust laws designed to restore the forms of early economy.

Thus in effect, industry and agriculture were nationalized in operation and interdependence; wages, hours, and working conditions in each region affected wages, hours, and working conditions in all regions; and the national consequences of panics or dislocations in economy were intensified. It became scarcely possible for any section or staple industry to enjoy prosperity and provide full employment while other sections or industries were in a state of depression.

Individuals in Economy Are
Organized in Associations.

Interwoven with these changes in economic practice was the organization of participants in production, within industry and outside—manufacturers, industrial workers, and farmers. Owners and managers of productive and distributive establishments were associated immediately by specialties—manufacturers of electrical supplies and retail merchants, for example; and they were affiliated vertically and horizontally through local, state, and national associations and chambers of commerce. In the field of labor a similar process of organization occurred, until the major portion of the workers in large staple enterprises were organized in independent and company unions. Less effectively, but still on a considerable scale, especially with state and federal assistance, agricultural producers were drawn together in cooperative marketing and credit associations, local and nation-wide in scope. No comprehensive figures are available, but it is safe to say that only in isolated and special cases do individuals in the productive and distributive processes stand alone, unaffiliated with any economic association, and completely free to determine their own working rules and to dictate the terms of their own contracts or managerial operations. And steadily through the years have been developed codes of fair practices limiting the range and types of individual activities and opportunities that prevailed when the philosophy of public education was first formulated.

Family Economy Is Disintegrating.

No less significant for national culture, for the fortunes of individuals, and for education, was the loosening of the family bonds that existed when industry and agriculture were localized and more or less self-sufficing. For centuries the household had been the center of education in the practical arts and the humanities—a school of mutual aid and the social virtues indispensable to the State. However intense the struggle for existence, mutual aid, collective responsibility, and individual sacrifice had marked the economy of the family. It was not without reason that Aristotle, writing long before the birth of Christ, started his immortal treatise on Politics with a consideration of the domestic unit, for, he said, "the family is the association established by nature for the supply of men's everyday wants, and the members of it are called by Charandas 'companions of the cupboard' and by Epimendes the Cretan 'companions of the manger.'" Nor is it to be overlooked that the very term "economics" is derived from the Greek word meaning "the management of household affairs."

As long as the family was self-sufficing and intact, its members assumed responsibilities for education and group welfare, according to capacity; they shared food, clothing, and shelter; they perished together in floods, droughts, famines, and wars. But when machines and industrial specialization disintegrated the household and destroyed the homestead arts, they drew members of the domestic

unit, young and old, into factories and other enterprises
beyond the hearth. Although the family remained, its
ancient economic ties were broken. Often the "fluidity of labor" enabled its members to escape entirely from
home and from responsibilities; in millions of cases, even
the mothers, from primitive times guardians of the household arts and sacrificial conservators of family goods,
became wage-earners in shops, factories, and offices. Hence
old reliance upon the family as a guarantee of security and
as a generator of moral forces steadily weakened. Long
ago educational administration felt the shock of this transformation. A restatement of educational obligations must
reckon with its relevant facts.

The Functions of Government Touch
All Branches of Life and Economy.

With the mechanization of economy and the loosening
of the family bonds ran the multiplication of government
functions and services, to which brief reference has been
made. These functions now touch every branch of industry, agriculture, finance, the management of natural resources, employment, morals, and security. They go far
beyond the crude protection of life and property. Some
are regulatory—factory legislation, control of utilities, and
rules pertaining to industries affected with public interest.
Other public functions are stimulative—tariffs, subsidies,
bounties, and government purchasing and lending. In
certain fields government has entered operating economy—
the Panama Canal, the Tennessee Valley development, par-
cels post, postal savings, water works, parks, forests, docks,
harbor facilities. In many relations government cooper-
ates with private enterprise—the Boulder Dam power
project, the New York subway system, and rural electrifi-
cation (grid projects). With disintegration of town and

village sufficiency, with the merging of the family and the community into a specialized and integrated economy, governments—federal, state, and local—assumed social obligations on a huge scale: institutional care, old age pensions, and insurance against dependency and unemployment.

The Growth of Public Functions Is Cumulative.

The origins of the expansion in public functions may be traced back into the nineteenth century, and in some cases, beyond. Its municipal manifestations reached a high point by 1914; its state forms, in many respects, ran parallel and widened as the nineteenth century merged into the twentieth; federal functions, in some features, date from the adoption of the Constitution but, in their proliferation, mark the advance of the twentieth century. The revolutionary character of the contrast is sharply illustrated by a comparison of President Van Buren's refusal to lift a finger in the panic of 1837 with the assumption of heavy obligations by President Hoover in the crisis of 1929, and still heavier obligations by President Roosevelt in 1933.

It Is Not the Work of Any Single Political Party.

This growth of public functions has been a process of accretion and accumulation. No political party has deliberately and consistently favored it. No political party in practice has deliberately and consistently opposed it. A study of the votes in state legislatures and in the Congress of the United States shows that on most of the measures adding to public obligations political parties have themselves been divided. The benefits, therefore, cannot be ascribed to any party; nor the evils. Indeed the growth of public functions has gone on despite the fortunes of parties and leaders. With something like the inexorableness of a natural process, it has accompanied the development of American society over a long period of time, gaining momentum as the nineteenth century turned into the twentieth. Critics may condemn; admirers may praise. The fact remains. And even the severest critics make discriminations; they would preserve some of these functions while abandoning others.

No Sharp Line Divides Public and Private Economy.

So deeply embedded in the texture of economy and social life are these government functions that no sharp line divides public and private economy. Theory may draw it in words; practice and knowledge cannot discover it in the conduct of affairs. Thus a transformation in the very structure of American society must be recorded since the establishment of educational philosophy and practice in the age of Jacksonian democracy. At the opening of that period American society was relatively simple. With slight sacrifice of truth it could be said that it was actually governed by Adam Smith's "mechanical principles" (see page 38). In our age, on the other hand, society is a complication of individual activities and social relations. The individual remains, and individual virtues are still indispensable. But all individuals must in cold fact operate their economies and conduct their lives under what John R. Commons calls "the Working Rules of Going Concerns, taking many forms and names, such as the common law, statute law, shop rules, business ethics, business methods, norms of conduct, and so on, which these governing or regulating groups of associated individuals have laid down for guidance of transactions." If anything is known about the actual nature of human affairs and human relations, this much is known: All educational philosophies and activities designed to prepare pupils for the real world of going concerns must take account of it and cope with its thrusts and demands. Failure to do so means an avoidance of truth as well as of obligations.

The Scientific Method Dissolves Old Social Dogmas.

The validity of what has just been said rests upon another positive development that has taken place since the advent of Jacksonian democracy and the early formulations of educational philosophy, namely, the wide application of the scientific method to the study of human affairs. In essence the application of the scientific method means the utmost possible emancipation from the dictates of *a priori* or dogmatic notions, whether of theological revelation, Colbertian mercantilism, Ricardian individualism, or Marxian communism. Correlatively it means an effort to know things as they have been and now are, without reference to preconceived dogmas respecting the way they ought to have been and to be. In short, the scientific method fostered by learning brought the keen edge of analysis to bear on the habitual assumptions of the period which saw the establishment of public education.

The Social Sciences Present Huge Bodies of New Knowledge.

Without doubt those who apply the scientific method are human and subject to error, but by employing engines of authentication and cross-verification they have created immense bodies of knowledge which command authority through the consensus of competence. The fruits of their labors are represented by whole libraries of works written since the age of Andrew Jackson—critical and documented history, anthropology, political economy, political science, sociology, psychology, and institutional behavior. Despite all conflicts in social theory and many shortcomings in presentation, these branches of knowledge are so solidly established that theorists and practitioners in government, economy, social relations, and education are compelled to use them, unless content to be futile or utopian. Although the social sciences have not attained, and in the nature of things cannot attain, the exactness of generalization reached by the physical sciences, they are as indispensable to efficient individual conduct and social practice as technology is to machine industry; and reliance on them will increase as society grapples resolutely with its problems and potentialities.

The Course of Foreign Relations Changes.

While drawing attention to changes in domestic affairs that followed the original establishment of public education in the United States, it is equally imperative to record alterations in the posture of international affairs; for at bottom domestic and foreign affairs are parts of the same thing. Even a superficial comparison of the world map today with that of 1850 reveals aspects of the transformation. After 1850 the systematization of the old commercial rivalry, known for convenience as imperialism, took form and profoundly influenced the course of European and American policy. In the latter part of the nineteenth century, after the closing of the frontier, the Government of the United States waged war on Spain, annexed overseas territories, threw its weight on the side of commercial expansion, entered more extensively into the competitions of the great powers, and began to take part in world councils for the determination of international relations.

Sponsors of American Expansion
Promise Prosperity and Security.

The economic side of the American adventure in world affairs was summarily stated by Senator Albert J. Beveridge, one of the leaders in bringing it about: "American factories are making more than the American people can use; American soil is producing more than they can consume. Fate has written our policy for us; the trade of the world must and shall be ours. And we will get it as our mother [England] has told us how. We will establish trading-posts throughout the world as distributing-points for American products. We will cover the ocean with our merchant marines. We will build a navy to the measure of our greatness. Great colonies governing themselves, flying our flag and trading with us, will grow about our posts of trade." Later this policy was supplemented by a program for fostering a huge export of capital to enable foreign countries to buy American products and thus enlarge the outlets for "surpluses."

But the World Outlook Is Clouded.

That these policies failed to provide anything like adequate outlets for American "surpluses" needs no demonstration in detail. The state of American agriculture after 1920 and of American industry after 1929 makes proof superfluous. Meanwhile there have been disturbing events in world affairs, European and Oriental: the renewal of imperial rivalries, the rearmament race and the reappearance of war menaces, accompanied by the resolve of the

United States to stay out of the next conflict, as expressed in drastic neutrality legislation. These events give a world setting for the United States in 1937 which is unlike anything hitherto experienced. If the choice is to enter the next World War, if and when it opens, there can be no doubt about its shattering repercussions in American society. Judging by the regimentation of mind and economy that prevailed after America's entrance into the last European conflict, and by the upheavals that followed it, the shape of coming things, in case of participation in another war, wears appalling aspects. If, on the other hand, the decision is to stay out of war, and to accept the derangements of commerce connected with mandatory neutrality, then thorough-going adjustments of internal economy become imperative.

A Call for New Foreign Policy Comes.

In any event, imperialism and government promotion of commercial enterprise did not provide full outlets for American "surpluses," any more than free land solved the problem of poverty after 1862. There is no reason to suppose that participation in another war would bring more than a temporary "relief," if that. Hence America now confronts an imperative question in domestic and foreign policies. It may be briefly stated in the following form: What is to be done with the "surpluses" of American industry and agriculture, and what foreign and domestic policies are appropriate? Iron circumstances have provided a new configuration of interests within which this dilemma is to be resolved, and educational leadership, in common with all other forms of leadership, must face it in adjusting thought and practice to contemporary demands. Resort to epithets "nationalist" and "internationalist" is neither appropriate nor helpful.

These Transformations Provide a Novel
Setting for Educational Planning.

It is evident from this summary that the movement of interests and ideas has created for educational philosophy and practice, a social context which is fundamentally different in many respects from the setting in which the founders of the public schools worked. American society is no longer a fairly simple order of agriculture and manufacturing, in which prudence, talents, industry, and thrift are automatically assured places and achievements. It is instead a highly complicated association controlled by a close mechanism of working rules, public and private, which must be effectively observed to assure anything like an adequate functioning of either economy or government. The opportunities and responsibilities of the individual in this society are correspondingly complex. Coping with them calls for specialized knowledge, and for a strong spirit of good-will. Simple confidence in the assertion of rights against society, which characterized the nineteenth century, is no longer sufficient. It is now everywhere recognized that rights asserted are futile unless accompanied by the policy and the competence necessary to maintain the kind of society in which rights proclaimed can be enjoyed.

The Task of Recasting Educational Philosophy in
New Terms Falls on Educational Leadership.

Such being the case, it follows that American society is not one in which the problems of government, economy, and social living have been solved for all time, leaving to education the simple function of disseminating fixed doctrines and the knowledge of the practical arts—or of serving the authorities immediately in power. On the contrary, it is a society which confronts basic issues at home and in foreign relations, even the fundamental issue of preserving the democratic processes themselves. In such a society education has creative as well as conservative functions and obligations of the highest order.

If it is said that education must merely follow the State, then the question arises, What is the State? The President of the United States at the moment? The majority in Congress? The majority in the state legislature or the city council? The governor or the mayor? Directors of farm organizations, trade unions, chambers of commerce, or any minority that can exert pressure on the schools?

This question surely answers itself, at least for all who are not prepared to throw overboard the cultural obligations of education and accept the dictation of immediate political officers or special interests. To be sure educational leadership does not and cannot ignore other forms of leadership in American society; nor does it arrogate to itself infallibility, even within its own sphere. But the functions of education in maintaining and enriching civilization distinguish it from instant political and economic activities, and impose upon it responsibilities that are wider and deeper than any mere professional concern. Those responsibilities are difficult to know and discharge. That goes without saying. But loyalty to the knowledge and aspiration associated with education requires an exploration and definition of its obligations, with all the powers of mind and understanding available. Belittling our capacities in the presence of duty, as John Morley said long ago, is as indefensible as fostering an unwarranted egotism.

Summary of the Background.

Public education is anchored in the nature of civilization as unfolded. It is thus closely associated with the ideals, policies, and institutions of government and economy, as well as the arts and sciences. Although some forms of private education may be far removed from the hard world of practice, public education can maintain no such isolation. Many professional representatives, it is true, may properly concentrate on schoolroom procedure, methods, and testing, but the leaders who determine the content and objectives of instruction must work under the immediate impacts of society—its needs, drives, and demands. The degree to which these constructive organizers are aware of, and informed respecting, the historical and contemporary forces pressing upon the schools, may be said to mark the state of their preparation for effective leadership.

Distinguished founders of the Republic deemed education indispensable to the perpetuity of the nation, to the realization of its ideals, and to the smooth functioning of American society. Under the impetus of this deep conviction, they explored the nature of education, made plans, and urged the establishment of institutions of learning appropriate to the American setting. Having waged war in a common cause, having established a Constitution to form a more perfect union, they laid heavy emphasis on the utility of education in overcoming the disruptive tendencies of particularism and preparing the people for the discharge of national obligations. In so doing they displayed profound insight into the forces requisite to the creation and operation of a great society. They did more. They set an impressive example to all those of succeeding generations who are called upon to make constructive efforts in education on a large scale and under grand conceptions of public policy. They demonstrated for all time that education is an enterprise worthy of the highest talents, inviting the boldest thought, and forever linked with the cultural destiny of the nation.

In the second period of American development public education was deemed no less important. Indeed it was so highly esteemed that immense sacrifices were made to secure its establishment. But this period was marked by an intense reaction against the cultural outlook of the founders, by emphasis on the sovereignty of the states, by laissez faire in Federal policy, by the march of equalitarian democracy, and by a passionate individualism. Not until the close of the civil conflict in 1865 was it clearly decided that the Union could survive the action of these centrifugal forces. In other words, the second stage in the growth of American society presented many aspects of a sharp antithesis to the first; and they were stamped on educational theory and practice.

Yet the antithesis did not wholly prevail. The unity of the nation was preserved, as the founders of the Republic had hoped. But it was democratized, in a way which few of them contemplated. Liberty was widened by the abolition of slavery. A profound stimulus was given to individual enterprise, as education equalized opportuntiy for training. And by a strange fate the energies of individual enterprise thus trained in schools under state and local auspices, and released in action, swiftly rounded out the continent, laced all parts of the country together by systems of transportation, and bound its sections and industries into a national economy. Meanwhile agencies of communication merged provincial ideas and thought in a larger consensus, such as the founders of the Republic had sought to create.

So it has come about that public education, as in 1789, is once more concerned with national economy and interests, despite its origins in state and local enterprise. Whereas George Washington once urged the promotion of education by national action, states and communities now turn to the Federal Government for aid in carrying on the work which they insisted upon starting under their own control. Through the influence of common ideals, methods, and associations, public education itself draws into a unity of thought and purpose which is nation-wide in its reach. Even in the most independent communities the impacts of national economy are felt; and the social studies which the schools teach are of necessity deeply concerned with that economy. The age-long conflict between centralism and particularism, between collective interest and private interest, has not closed, and cannot be closed; but upon educational leadership devolves a certain responsibility for keeping that conflict within the bounds of exact knowledge, good-will, and the democratic process, and of contributing to the formulation of wise and humane decisions.

So viewed, the association of educational history with the encompassing history of American civilization is not a form of antiquarianism and dust-sifting. On the contrary by this process alone does it seem possible to obtain sure guidance in the formulation of an educational policy corresponding to the realities of the living present, now rising out of the past.

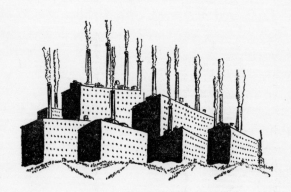

VI.

The Nature of Educa-
tion and Its Obligations.

When all that is associated with education as philosophy
and reality is brought under review, it presents two phases
which, though inseparable, may be called for convenience
intrinsic and *extrinsic*. While education constantly touches
the practical affairs of the hour and day, and responds
to political and economic exigencies, it has its own treasures heavy with the thought and sacrifices of the centuries. It possesses a heritage of knowledge and heroic
examples—accepted values stamped with the seal of per-
manence. Yet it is more than the inanimate record of
tradition, more than books, maps, pictures, models, and
methods of instruction. Education finds expression in the
living personalities connected with it, in the relations of
board and administration, in the associations of teachers
and pupils, in attitudes, bearings, and skills, in all the
nobler impulses of the humanities which are sustaining
forces of society. Forever affiliated with education, in
varying degrees of intensity, is the inscrutable urge of
aspiration and creative intelligence which gives elevation to
daily duties and seeks the improvement of the heritage. It
guards those virtues of the race that are vouchsafed to the
humblest—industry, patience, self-denial, and consideration for others, and at the same time it stimulates the more
imperial gifts of imagination, originality, and invention
by which the treasures of mankind are enlarged and enriched. Wielding no weapons of sheer power, claiming
no pomp and circumstance of State, education nourishes

the underlying values upon which State and Society depend for their existence—values which outlast transformations in the working rules of government and economy, and offer promises of humane reconstruction in times of crisis and threatened dissolution. Beyond question, the members of the teaching profession do not claim to be adequately prepared by natural talents or by training for the weighty tasks imposed upon them by education. Nor does any Hippocratic oath bind them into a single fraternity committed with whole heart to the ideals of their own heritage. But even an elementary knowledge of the history of education, from crude drawings on the walls of paleolithic caves to the complicated activities of the modern university, vests in them a fiduciary trust meritorious in itself and to be protected against mere coercion and expediency. This trust remains a center of interest and affection when that aspect of education, called extrinsic, is drawn into consideration and the obligations of the schools to government, economy, and society are determined and assumed.

The Intrinsic Features of Education.

No sharp line can be traced between the inmost substances of education and the external circumstances that influence it and call upon its leadership for services. Yet there is a center of gravity in education—a treasury of knowledge, aspirations, and values—that endures and is to be cherished against mere expediency. This heritage is old in its origins and still ever new in contemporaneous thought. It contains some features peculiar to America and some that are common to education in all ages and all countries, however carried on—under domestic, private, religious, independent, or public auspices. These features are indeed primordial for civilization. They represent values which the sponsors of democracy from antiquity to modern times have deemed essential to humane living and to effective self-government.

This is no place to attempt a distillation of forty centuries of educational thought and aspiration, even were the powers to undertake it at command. But stress must be laid on the intrinsic and enduring features of education. Otherwise they may be neglected amid the pressures of immediate demands upon the schools; and encouragement may be given to the menacing conception that education is nothing in itself, is a mere servant of triumphant power —political, military, or economic.

It is obvious, and still must be emphasized, that education has obligations attached to the profession. The teacher is not a soldier, a lawyer, a physician, a businessman, a farmer, or an industrial worker. Other callings have their responsibilities. Teaching has the responsibilities of its commitments. In its heritage is knowledge—of the great classics deemed appropriate for instruction in the schools, of educational philosophy from Plato through Rousseau and Froebel to the latest pathbreakers, of the scientific works employed in the several branches of learning, and of the technical works on method and practice. It is the duty of teachers, according to their powers, to master as much of this knowledge as they can.

Above all, education has obligations to truth in itself and for its own sake—obligations to seek it, defend it, and make humane use of it. Education must keep alive memories, linking the past with the present and tempering the sensations of the hour by reference to the long experiences of the race. It must kindle and feed the imagination, by bringing past achievements of the imagination into view and indicating how new forms of science, art, invention, and human association may be called into being. Education must foster aspiration—the desire to be more, to acquire greater skill and knowledge, and to create. It must cherish beauty as a value in itself and as contributing to mental health, power, and pleasure, as adding rewards to labor and delight to life. Concerned with truth and the great powers of mind and heart, education is bound to assert the liberty in which they may flourish, to quicken minds, to encourage searching and inventiveness, to employ tolerance and the judicial spirit, to inculcate habits of gentleness and justice. On these considerations education has no monopoly, to be sure, but its intrinsic obligations fall within the broad field thus laid out.

Guardians of Educational Values Have Their Professional Obligations.

Protecting and enriching the intrinsic powers of education is a task for all who are concerned with education, whether as teachers, administrators, or lay persons outside the school system. It has been their task since the dawn of civilization, perhaps earlier. There is ground for faith that the task will never be abandoned. The lamps of learning were kindled long ago. They have burned in caves and log cabins, as well as in great buildings erected by wealth and power. We may be sure that no barbarism, new or old, can extinguish them forever. Should society enter upon an age of scorn and neglect, even should the wrath of men tear down the very walls of school buildings, as it burned the library of Alexandria, should one or all these lamps be put out, some hands will rekindle them, and will defend them for a better day. While paying due heed to the exigencies of times and occasions, educational leadership true to its trust must continue to uphold the intrinsic values of education.

Potentials as Well as Heritage
Enter into Consideration.

But a statement of what has been done and is being done by education is not enough. We have before us a body of thought and practice bearing the name of education. That must be examined. We have before us current theory and usage. With them we must be familiar. Still another step must be taken. We do not work in the past or for the mere ends of the present. By the very nature of our obligations, we are compelled to face the future. All planning and action have reference to it. We cannot plan for the past, nor act in it. The public schools are concerned with the coming generations, not with the past and the passing. It is in the years ahead, not in any ages gone, iron or golden, that these generations will live their lives, carry on their work, assert their rights, and discharge their duties.

The Program of Education
Is Never Completed.

By this conception of education, the very idea of completed formalism and perfect practice handed down by the past is ruled out. Teachers are not pedagogues. They cannot discharge their obligations by saying to pupils: "There is your Virgil; in the corner are the birches; learn your Virgil." Society will not let them rest content with such a procedure, even if they are inclined to do so. Nor are they so inclined. Moved by the ancient command to search out all things under the sun and by the spirit of science to seek new knowledge endlessly, teachers are pioneers, not mere camp followers. Their task is not limited to preserving and passing on a heritage of knowledge and treasured experience; they must take account of advancing knowledge, add to it when they can, sift and create as well as accumulate.

It Grows with the Growth of Humanity.

Unless they do this, they fall under the dead hand; knowledge will advance without them, in spite of them; and society, finding death, not life, in the schools, will withdraw support. Or perhaps society itself, deriving no nourishment from education and ceasing to grow, will ossify, if not disintegrate. Hence, educators cannot abide by the record alone. It unfolds in their keeping. They too are stirred by the questing spirit, spurred by the examples of the great thinkers and doers whose record they keep, stimulated by the currents of thought in society itself. So moved, they are literally compelled to enlarge their own powers, to enrich their own minds, and ever anew to chart their own obligations. Like the human history in which it is applied, the program of education is never completed. The things that education can do are thus as pressing as the things which it has done and does do. For all we know, until we have tried to the utmost, the work ahead may be more important. Hence any definition of education calls for a consideration of what may be done in its name, as well as what has been done and is now being carried on.

Its Source Is Life, Not Merely
Books and Laws.

Experience, the great jurist Oliver Wendell Holmes has said, is the life of the law; no matter how much at times and places formalists seek to bind its trunk and stunt its growth. Having in front of him the written Constitution of the United States and the records telling of its history, another jurist, Thomas M. Cooley, declared: "We may think that we have the Constitution all before us; but for practical purposes the Constitution is that which the government in its several departments and the people in the performance of their duties as citizens recognize and respect as such; and nothing else is. . . . Cervantes says: 'Everyone is the son of his own works.' This is more emphatically true of an instrument of government than it can possibly be of a natural person."

We may have before us all the volumes ever written on the intrinsic features of education, all the great treatises on methods and procedures, all the curricula, and the relevant statutes, orders, and decrees; yet all of education is not in them. To paraphrase Judge Cooley, education is that which living educators in official positions, and citizens who give their life and thought to the promotion of education, recognize and respect as such. How could it be otherwise? If, as the poet has said, dead but sceptered sovereigns rule us from their tombs, even they rule only through the thought, memories, and aspirations of the living. Education not only preserves and teaches history; it makes history—in some way, large or small, according to the conceptions and powers of the educators.

Education Embraces Knowledge,
Training, and Aspiration.

Against such a background, nothing less, must any wide-reaching statement of education for our times be made. Well aware that there is something arbitrary in all definitions, we may nevertheless make the attempt. The primary business of education, in effecting the promises of American democracy, is to guard, cherish, advance, and make available in the life of coming generations the funded and growing wisdom, knowledge, and aspirations of the race. This involves the dissemination of knowledge, the liberation of minds, the development of skills, the promotion of free inquiries, the encouragement of the creative or inventive spirit, and the establishment of wholesome attitudes toward order and change—all useful in the good life for each person, in the practical arts, and in the maintenance and improvement of American society, as our society, in the world of nations. So conceived, education seems to transcend our poor powers of accomplishment. It does in fact, if perfection be expected; but such is the primary business of public education in the United States; theory supports it; practice inadequately illustrates and confirms it.

Knowledge of the Practical and Social Arts.

The knowledge disseminated by the schools has been classified according to a scheme extending from "essentials" to "ornaments." Although fallacious, the classification is convenient for the moment. In the first class come all those subjects of instruction deemed by general consensus to be necessary to the practical arts, namely reading, writing, arithmetic, and the elements of natural science. These branches of learning are regarded as independent of time, place, and circumstance—above and beyond all partial and partisan interests. In the second class come subjects respecting the "working rules of society" in both public and private aspects. Although they have been divided into rules of government on the one side and rules of private economy on the other—political science and economics—their relations in practice admit of no clean-cut division. Within this class is embraced knowledge of political ideas and institutions, government, liberty, and the processes of democracy—proposal, discussion, adoption, and appraisal. Here falls knowledge of institutions, ideas, and practices, private and public, especially connected with the production and distribution of wealth —using wealth to include material goods and well-being.

Knowledge of the Funded Wisdom and
Aspirations of the Race.

In the third class of knowledge disseminated by the schools are the literature of imagination and aspiration and the so-called fine arts, which are often regarded by the thoughtless as "ornamental." In truth they are not mere refinements of life. They bear upon and are interwoven with all the technical and practical arts supposed to be necessary to the very existence of society. They, no less than the practical arts, serve to distinguish civilization from barbarism. Indeed, it is possible to imagine a society of people well-fed and well-governed, and still devoid of all the knowledge and interests that make human life worth living. Even the maintenance of economy and government depends upon other things than mere technical knowledge and competence. In truth, the distinction between the fine and the practical arts is superficial and unreal; a bolt of cloth, a piece of furniture, and a steel bridge may be designed with a severe eye to use, and in that functional perfection be a superb manifestation of "fine" art.

Without the literature and the arts which keep alive imagination and aspiration, which reflect taste and give enjoyment, industry would be on a low level and government would partake of the culture of the barracks. Without the ethical and esthetic aspirations reflected in the great literature of the race—embodying its funded and accumulating wisdom—government, industry, and even the "fine" arts would be without form, spirit, and force. Uncontrolled by ethics and esthetics, the practical arts may destroy civilization. Apart from them civilization is inconceivable and impossible.

The Practical, Social, and "Fine" Arts Are
All Essential Parts of Education.

Hence, while the knowledge which the schools disseminate may be classified for convenience into subjects treating of the practical arts, the working rules of society, literature, and the fine arts, as if there were here a scheme of values to be arranged in a hierarchy, the classification and hierarchy are false to reality. All these values are necessary to a civilization, and each is essential to the existence and development of the others. All must be brought within any plan of education designed to disseminate knowledge useful in the practical arts, the good life, and the maintenance and improvement of society. In stating its position, educational leadership, if loyal to its heritage and to the society that sustains the school, must discard the conception of a hierarchy of values and insist on the preservation and advancement of all these branches of knowledge and interest. Any curtailments which economic stringency may require must be proportionately applied.

Knowledge Alone Is Not Enough—
Ethics Is Indispensable.

In the definition of public education for the United States thus generalized, it is evident, the dissemination of knowledge is not the whole business of education. More elusive elements are included. The nature of the knowledge to be disseminated is qualified by the condition, "useful in the good life and in the maintenance and improvement of American society." Both ethics and the nature of American civilization are drawn into immediate and inescapable consideration. Knowledge alone does not present imperatives of conduct; nor kindle aspiration for the good life; nor necessarily exemplify it. Knowledge of chemistry may be employed to poison a neighbor as well as to heal the sick. Knowledge of banking may be used to exploit and wreck banks as well as in banking practices of unquestioned social advantage. There is nothing in a chemical fact, or in a financial fact, which necessarily instructs the learner in the right use of it. Commands relative to usage come from other sources—from the funded wisdom and aspirations of the race, whatever elements of expediency may enter into the account. Ethics is, therefore, not a side issue with education as here conceived, but is a central concern—a concern that gives direction to the spread of knowledge. The selection of knowledge to be disseminated and emphasis placed on courses of study are ethical choices, not categorical commands arising solely out of knowledge or out of studies hitherto pursued.

Educators Carry Ethical Responsibilities.

The statement that ethics is a fundamental concern of education rests upon the intrinsic heritage of education as well as upon immediate experience. The acknowledged leaders and sponsors of education in all ages have been in fact ethical teachers. Their theories and practices have centered upon enduring good, not upon evil or indifference to evil. Even those leaders of education who have laid emphasis on the scientific method as a correct instrument for securing accurate knowledge concerning matters physical and human have proceeded upon some ethical assumptions, some conceptions of things worth while, either tacit or explicit. No educational leader has ever held that teachers may properly organize themselves into a band of robbers for the purpose of employing knowledge in preying upon society. The very idea is odious to educational thought. A declaration of ethical purpose is, therefore, inherent in education as theory and practice.

The Classics of Learning Are Ethical.

Moreover, in the funded wisdom and knowledge which education cherishes and expounds are the classical works of the world's ethical teachers. Education would cease to be education if it ruled out of consideration Plato's Republic, the Bible, or the writings of all such thinkers as Thomas Aquinas, John Ruskin, or Ralph Waldo Emerson. Ironical as it may seem, if society were stripped of ethical cement it would offer nothing to bandits and robbers. Even they thrive on the ethics of others; for ethical forces are indispensable to the existence of every society, primitive or civilized. By the examples of leaders, by the content of the heritage committed to it, education derives from ethics and is bound to make ethics a controlling and in-spiriting concern of its continuing interest.

Education Includes the Training of Body and Spirit.

It is not merely with the transmission of knowledge that education is deeply concerned. The functions of the schools are not fully described by a summary of programs, curricula, and methods. No written or spoken words do, or can, completely convey the meaning of education as the day-to-day living force that it is in fact and may be—in the transactions of the classroom, in the relations of teacher and pupil, in the associations of pupil and pupil, and in the experiences of the library and athletic field. Here are exchanges, bearings, and influences too subtle for logical expression and exact measurement. Yet we cannot doubt their existence, at least those of us who recall our own educational experiences and see teachers at work. Here, in the classroom, the auditorium, laboratory, and gymnasium, are in constant operation moral and cultural forces just as indispensable to civilization as knowledge or any material elements—indeed primordial in nature and the preconditions for the civilized uses of material things. We cannot set them forth in mathematical tables, nor in parallel columns; we can merely hint at their more evident characteristics.

In classrooms, day by day, thousands of teachers come into contact with children of all sorts and conditions, races and nationalities, religious and ethical backgrounds. From homes of every kind—those broken by disputes of parents, wracked by the uncertainties and distresses of poverty and unemployment, no less than those tranquil in management and supplied by the means of material well-being. From homes poor in spirit, devoid of art, without books, without interest in things above the routine of living and the babble of gossip, thin in culture, perhaps tinged with crime, beset by distempers of mind, no less than from the homes that represent the best in American life. Here in the classrooms is manifest the gamut of American civilization.

The school is not set apart from society on an academic hill. Teachers are more constantly and intimately associated with, or at least brought into contact with, things great and small in American society, high and mean, than the members of any other profession, public or private. They must grapple with the distempers which society and individual conduct generate, while seeking to preserve and to disseminate the best that is in its culture. The schools deal with the enduring stresses of human life, as well as with its enduring values.

And this they do through the living contacts of teachers and the taught, pupil and pupil. Discipline and freedom, authority and responsibility, helpfulness and challenge are made living in the spoken word, in attitude, gesture, and behavior. When the shortcomings of education are admitted, when the pettiness or incompetence of this or that teacher is conceded, we have only to imagine what American society would be if all public school buildings were razed and all public education abandoned. This is not to say that there was nothing good before public education was established, but that public education maintains and demonstrates human relations indispensable to the good life in itself and to the perdurance and functioning of a democratic society.

Education Fosters the Social
Virtues by Example.

In the classroom and on the playground, from hour to hour and year to year, are in fact exemplified the better virtues of the enlarged family. Order and play are balanced, mutual aid and mutual respect are promoted, displays of unleashed passion are discredited and discouraged, and the give and take of the good life are illustrated. Habits of reasoned obedience, illuminated by knowledge of consequences, are inculcated. The good and the beautiful, without which both the fine arts and the practical arts are poverty-stricken and lampless, are incorporated in conduct, and in visible signs—books and maps, pictures and flowers, or drawings and designs. Even in the poorest and most barren schoolroom in the poorest and most barren community, education in form and practice rises to some height above the lowest common denominators of the district; not high enough, by confession, yet to some height. Here, so to speak, is a little focus of civilization, a symbol of its values, an embodiment of its aspirations in things, words, and deeds. Here the values of society appear in miniature, in microcosm. Here is woven during the formative years of youth a texture of knowledge, habit, aspiration, and mutual respect which aids in holding society together, counteracts the divisive forces of personal, political, and economic rivalry, and helps to sustain humanity amid all the forms of untried being through which it must pass. Politics, economics, finance, administration, amusements, the practical arts, wars, and even social cyclones are phases of life; education is concerned with the whole of life and the best of it. It has been so conceived; it is now so conceived; however faulty and defective the personalities and procedures associated with it. Thousands of schools in the United States, no doubt, fall far below the ideal standards, but that fact is merely evidence of the need for heroic efforts in the direction of improvement, not a repudiation of educational obligations.

Education Is Committed to the Maintenance and Improvement of American Society.

Beyond the fiduciary trust vested in it, beyond the heritage of ideas and practices which it deems *intrinsic* values, education has other obligations, called for convenience *extrinsic*. It is committed to the maintenance and improvement of American society as now constituted and unfolding, and to the use of knowledge and the practical arts in a manner conducive to these ends. Outside of society, neither education nor individual liberty nor the practical arts can flourish. Those who would make a new social order can scarcely imagine that there is no good whatever in the present array of things, or in the men and women out of which the new order is to be made. Nor will any who fain would limit education to the mere maintenance of the present order, assuming that it will not change in the future, be bold enough to say that it is utopia, a good without possibility of improvement, unmixed with evil. Although extremists may enjoy the luxury of such views, educators loyal to the knowledge which they are bound by their office to cherish cannot accept either of them as a dictate for educational theory and practice. If the past is all wrong, why study it or hope for the future? If the present is perfection, why the poverty and distresses of children in the schoolroom and the conflicts of party and interest outside? The sharp antithesis sometimes drawn between those who would have the schools create a new social order and those who would confine them to a mere defense of a *status quo* does not correspond to the known facts in the case.

This American Society Is Democratic.

The American society which education aids in maintaining and improving is by declaration, profession, and institutional organization a democratic society. It is such in truth, however far short of the ideal it may fall in many respects. It is not a monarchial society. It is not a military dictatorship. It has no legally established classes with prescriptive rights of government. Children are not assigned to a class by birth and held there till death. Its occupation, callings, and professions, and the opportunities to enter them are not wholly determined by accidents of birth. Gateways are not closed to talents by class law. Governments derive their just powers from the consent of the governed, and may be altered by the governed through the institutions of the law itself. The conflicts of society are to be resolved and its problems are to be handled by the processes of discussion and popular action.

It Repudiates Government
by Sheer Force.

To this type of society the American people are committed by their heritage, by long practice, and by their sense of values. Other types have existed and now exist. Whatever their diversities in external forms, they are distinguished from the democratic society in their reliance on force for the establishment of government and the direction of domestic policy. The founders of the American Republic were familiar with them. They did not foresee the names that were to be applied to such societies in coming years; but they understood their essence, examined their merits, and rejected them. In establishing the Constitution of the United States by proposal, discussion, and popular decision, instead of resorting to force, as advised by hot-heads, they broke the rhythm of history and correctly believed that they had set an example to mankind. The rejection of the lesson by other societies does not destroy the validity of the democratic process for the United States.

Democracy Nourishes the Free
Spirit of Science.

It may be said, however, that science and the scientific method which American education is bound to nourish are neutral, are indifferent to forms of government and the human values of democracy; in other words, that science may be monarchial, absolutist, or dictatorial in spirit. Men of science may, no doubt, bow to military and police force; they have often done just that. But science cannot employ all its powers in advancing the boundaries of knowledge, unless it is free to inquire and to expound its findings. The age-long conflict between science and authority demonstrates the truth of this proposition. It so happens, therefore, that the democratic processes of government are in harmony with the processes by which science proceeds from victory to victory. In American society citizens are free to inquire, to expound, to propose, and to appraise. Constitutional rules declare this freedom. Custom sanctions it. Institutions of government protect it. Among its many obligations, public education is charged with disseminating the knowledge and keeping alive the spirit necessary to the functioning of democracy. In so doing it helps to provide the conditions in which science can flourish and hence is loyal to the traditions and requirements of science.

Democracy Rests on Ideals, Institutions, and Economy.

The founders and early sponsors of American democracy were not under the illusion that it would work automatically by the mere counting of heads. Emphasis on eternal vigilance was as constant and as noteworthy as their championship of the democratic idea. They were poignantly aware that dictatorships had been established on popular distempers; that advocates of physical force had repeatedly appealed to passion for support. Democracy, they knew, rests upon a moral imperative that human life has a value in itself and cannot be used for purposes alien to humanity. Unremitting insistence upon this value, the development of this moral sense, is an obligation of all who teach and lead in democracy. Furthermore, loyalty to the institutions through which democracy functions, a willingness to abide by popular verdicts reached by due process, and to seek reversal, if desired, by the same methods—these too are essential elements of our democratic society. Yet, while laying emphasis on moral values and institutional loyalties, the founders and sponsors of American democracy also recognized the basic fact that the forms of property and the distribution of wealth—the ways and means of physical life—bear an inescapable relation to a democratic society, to its establishment and maintenance and to the adjustments requisite to its functioning.

The Philosophy of Democracy Enters into the Definition of Education.

In any realistic definition of education for the United States, therefore, must appear the whole philosophy and practice of democracy. Education cherishes and inculcates its moral values, disseminates knowledge necessary to its functioning, spreads information relevant to its institutions and economy, keeps alive the creative and sustaining spirit without which the letter is dead. The solution of specific problems of democracy devolves upon society. Education does not arrogate that function to itself. It does not claim either the competence or the sole power—legal or spiritual. But education does preserve and spread knowledge appropriate to the solution of specific problems, instills the disciplines essential to the acquisition of knowledge, describes the points of view from which problems are discussed, sets forth the assumptions and imperatives on which solutions depend, and in the classroom illustrates the spirit and procedure in which knowledge and reason are applied in coping with the adjustments of society. Whether these issues are related to political institutions, to finance and taxation, to industry, commerce, and agriculture, to public health, to the conservation and use of natural resources, to international relations and national defense, education is concerned with them. It presents knowledge relevant to them. It sets forth theories and values, from which they are approached. It illustrates in miniature, apart from the tempers and distempers of the political arena, the processes of enlightenment and discussion by which matured decisions are reached. Such is the obligation imposed on education by the democratic society in which it functions and which it serves. It cannot do less than assume the obligation, if loyal to its commitments. In so doing it acts not as a mere branch of government, as one profession among many engaged by government. It stands behind, exemplifies, and aids in sustaining all the processes of government and society.

The Assurance of Democratic Society No Longer Taken for Granted.

A sense of social responsibility has not been absent from education at any stage of its development; but for a long time the maintenance and improvement of American society were taken for granted as the automatic outcomes of individual activities. It was once assumed by some thinkers that the primary function of education was to train individuals so that they could rise into callings deemed higher, if not more lucrative. By other thinkers it was assumed that education must be concerned essentially with teaching the elements of the practical arts, and that the possessors of these elements would automatically find just and appropriate opportunities for employing them in the economy of society. For a period in American history, while the exploitation of the land and resources of the continental domain was proceeding and world trade expanding without apparent limits, these assumptions seemed founded on the realities of American practice. To be sure, some elements of history and civics were taught in this age of confidence, but instruction in these subjects was often so formal as to convey to pupils no sense of their worth or importance. It seems in harmony with the record to say that for nearly fifty years—from approximately 1870 to 1920—education took for granted the future of democratic society and, perhaps to a less extent, the eternal validity of the theory that both individual prosperity and social security were to be automatically assured by the free application of talents to personal ends.

Now the future of democratic society is challenged, not only in Europe and Asia, but in quarters by no means obscure or negligible in the United States. For educational leadership to blink that fact is to cast off the mandate of eternal vigilance and accept the facile optimism that paralyzes preventive measures. That this leadership is alive to the peril and to the opportunity has been demonstrated by professional actions in Washington, D. C., and in conventions of the Department of Superintendence of the National Education Association at St. Louis and of the Association at Portland in 1936. Once more, as in the early days of the Republic, the terms, conditions, and methods appropriate to the maintenance of democratic society swing into the center of educational interest. And with maintenance goes improvement.

Education Now Lays Emphasis on
Its Social Obligations.

As organized education turns to the future, then, it discards the theory of automatic democracy. It recognizes that rights to life, liberty, property, work, and the pursuit of happiness are shadows, unless those who claim the rights are competent and have the moral power necessary to the creation and maintenance of the social arrangements in which rights may be realized. If this obligation is staggering in its dimensions, educational leadership must accept it, acquire the knowledge, and put forth the sustained effort calculated to discharge it. Here, too, in facing the future, education reemphasizes the fact that it is not merely one profession among many, one branch of government among many. Its functions are all encompassing. Its duties are unique in their human aspects.

It Must Serve an Associational Economy.

Not only is the automatic theory of democracy challenged by events. The very economy in which it was once applied with assurance has been altered by events. So far as the major branches of manufacture, mining, and transportation are concerned, the associative system of the corporation has been substituted for individual ownership and management. To a less degree this rule holds for distributive branches of economy. In the field of industrial labor, freedom of individual movement is likewise limited by the associative efforts of independent and company unions. Even in agriculture, once the stronghold of individual independence, cooperative organizations gain strength, for marketing and credit purposes, and to some extent for buying. More and more, the fruit grower and the dairy farmer, for example, find themselves entering into and bound by collective marketing agreements, to which are generally attached, by law or custom, standards of quantity and quality.

It Must Prepare Youth for Associational
Life and Activities.

From this situation emerge stubborn facts with which educational theory and practice must reckon and cope. The overwhelming majority of the graduates of the schools in the cities who enter upon economic activities, will be employees of corporations, including the managerial, clerical, and industrial branches. If in business on their own account, they will be, in most cases, in corporate business or in enterprises to some extent associative in character. If independent in theory, they will have collective responsibilities in trade organizations and will be bound, more or less, by codes of fair practice. Graduates who enter employments below the managerial range will, in large proportion, find themselves in economic associations of some kind, carrying obligations and limitations. Specializing farmers, besides skill and resources, will need the knowledge and power requisite for the functioning of the associations through which marketing and price adjustments are effected. Thus school graduates will, in the main, whatever their careers, require knowledge of their associative obligations and the power to prevent such activities from degenerating into antisocial interests.

The business of society with which education is concerned is even more complicated than these few words indicate. The private organizations that occupy such a large area of economy have associations with one another; organized labor with organized industry; milk producers' societies with distributors; extractive industries with manufacturing industries, for example. The relations already established by practice are numerous and technical; on both sides special knowledge is employed.

Economic science sets forth this knowledge, with more or less completeness. Education disseminates it. The graduates of schools will need it, as certainly as technical proficiency, in the life and work upon which they are to enter. How are private economic associations formed? What are their present structures? How do they function? What are their rights and obligations? In what relation do the individual and the family stand to their forms and activities? If graduates from the schools are to have preparation for the real world of economic practice, education is compelled to take up these questions. To refuse this obligation would be to fall back upon formalism and unreality. To education alive to its responsibilities such withdrawal is impossible.

It Must Prepare Citizens for Participation in Associational Government.

The chart for educational planning is not yet completed. Surrounding these private associations is society, with government as its agency. Without the express or tacit consent of government these associations cannot come into being. Once in existence they raise problems for government, and bring pressure upon it. To an increasing degree, in the nation and in the states, irrespective of parties and politics, government is drawn into the relations and activities of associations. It prescribes a great body of law for them. It circumscribes their conflicts. It is subject to impulses from their interests. It establishes agencies for facilitating their inter-trade negotiations and adjustments. It imposes restraints on their practice. It is called upon to conserve the natural resources which they employ, and to define the "wise uses" of these resources. It has balances to maintain, endless adjustments to make.

Yet this government does not act in a vacuum under its own motion. Its officials are chosen directly or indirectly by enfranchised citizens. The public functions which they assume, the activities which they carry on, are the outcome of popular discussion and decision. So it happens then that citizens called upon to obey the law are the makers of law; and education is invited to do its part in preparing youth for a dual role—cooperation in obedience to law and cooperation in determining the forms and ends of law.

It Must Aid in Upholding
Social Values.

All society is concerned with these associations and with any government for the moment in power. Society also has values which are more than economic or political in nature, which are indeed indispensable to economic and political operations. Society is concerned with all of culture, with the moral code that holds its members together, as well as with the trade ethics of particular interests, and the fortunes of particular parties. Men and women need to live, but they can be poor in spirit, feeble in powers, hateful in disposition, low in civilization, and disruptive in influence, even if rich in material goods. No society can be founded on purely pecuniary standards, or can endure if so founded, or can give to life that richness of satisfaction and opportunity which makes it worth the living. And upon education is laid an obligation to see that the youth of the land possess the cultural values which sustain society, hold the conflicts of politics and economy within bounds, and enrich life itself.

Education Now Confronts New Functions in
Connection with Unemployed Youth.

In the facts just stated it is evident that the schools would carry heavy burdens even if American society were running smoothly, if all people were employed, if youth easily found opportunities commensurate with talents and competence. But we live in times of stress and tension. Millions are unemployed, and have been for years. Millions of boys and girls do not find opportunities beckoning as they leave the grade schools or the high schools. On the contrary, the labor saving machines and devices of industry diminish the proportion of human beings employed while increasing production. Not only does industry introduce rapid and bewildering shifts in the requirements of vocational analysis and guidance; it fails to expand employment rapidly enough to provide openings for a multitude of youth annually seeking engagements. As a result schools are often compelled to make provision for boys and girls for four or five years longer than was the case in the early years of this century. That is not all. Nor is it perhaps the most significant issue of machine industry, as thus far managed.

The pupils thus kept in the schools for more years and the teachers engaged in instructing them work under a strain of uncertainty, under the shadow of the terrifying thought that all the additional training may end in disappointment, in failure to find the opportunity for the release of youthful knowledge and energies. Industry and government tend to pass this responsibility to each other, without meeting its demands; they are also inclined to shift the burden to the schools without recognizing the limitations of these institutions, or providing them with appropriate resources. At all events, educational leadership is brought face to face with the stark question: What can and should the schools do to meet the unemployment problem that disturbs and baffles youth, to supply the vocational guidance appropriate to the tempo and characteristics of rapidly changing machine industries, and to familiarize pupils with the realities of the stern scene in front of them? This is not a question involving the mere routine of adjustment. It is a call for creative and constructive thought and action in education. It forces educational leaders to confront both industry and government and to find ways and means by which the three parties to the triangle may render to youth that justice without which education is in danger of becoming a mockery. Somewhere in this triangle public policy must provide an escape from the dilemma, or the deep forces of baffled energy may make a social explosion. Any conception of education that ignores this critical situation is false to its trust. And the effort of the schools to deal with it constructively lifts educational leadership out of the routine of pedagogy into the realm of bold and creative thinking which the founders of the Republic dared to enter.

*It Faces New Responsibilities for
the Education of Adults.*

Developments in machine industries and the deepening public interest in the quest for solutions of collective problems have also added obligations in adult education to the already heavy burdens of the schools. The period of youth is prolonged by the restriction of opportunities to enter upon life work. The high tempo of industry tends to discard men and women from occupations at or near the close of middle life. Public health measures, the curtailment of immigration, and a declining birth rate raise the proportion of adults in our society. The requirements of democratic self-government make it necessary for citizens to acquire a wider and deeper knowledge of public questions. Under the impact of these forces, schools are compelled to make extra provisions for youth approaching maturity and for men and women with leisure at their command—either forced or voluntary leisure. They are called upon to open their doors for the reasoned and sober discussion of public questions, to maintain forums in which the consideration of great issues may proceed.

All this, no doubt, is both fitting and proper—in keeping with and an expansion of the democratic process of self-government. It is not foreign to education. Yet it imposes upon leadership in school administration the duty of widening its horizon and grappling with intellectual and moral problems of the highest order. The issues so raised are certainly not less fundamental than those involved in freedom of the press and speech. Indeed by judicious administration, representing the general interest, school authorities may well supplement the discussions carried on by private agencies, such as the press and the radio, make their "public hearings" less partial and more informative, and contribute even more powerfully to the maintenance of democratic methods in government. As thus far developed under federal and state auspices, adult education in the public schools displays standards of administrative impartiality and local autonomy that promise to keep this channel of communication and inquiry free and wide open. The experiments already undertaken, refined and extended, will doubtless form a permanent part of educational duties in the United States.

So Defined, Education Is Distinguished from Propaganda.

By the conception herewith presented education is distinguished from propaganda, but the point deserves amplification. It is true that propaganda "in the broadest sense is the technique of influencing human action by the manipulation of representations" which may take "spoken, written, pictorial, or musical form." Yet in practice propaganda may be more accurately characterized as influencing human conduct by the manipulation of *mis*representations, or at least partial representations, for the advantage of special interests and with a view to commanding unquestioning obedience. There may be, and often is, a large element of truth in propaganda; without that element even the most ingenious propaganda fails.

When the purpose of a propaganda is to influence the whole of society, however, it means imposing upon all individuals slogans, formulas, and patterns of conduct in the interest of those in power at the moment or seeking to get into power. It is an instrument of a faction or a party. It is the foe of scientific exploration, of the open discussion required for the winnowing of truths particular and general, and of the progress that comes from the competition of new devices, ideas, processes, and practices. As applied to politics, it usually exalts in the name of the State the power of party against the individual, and demands servile acquiescence. In the form of Fascism, Individualism, or Marxism, propaganda assumes the infallibility of omniscience and pretends to possess a closed system of knowledge which enables adepts to prescribe the "right thing" in all circumstances and to guarantee the predicted outcome as good—immediately or in the long run. Whatever its guise, it belies single-hearted pursuit

[99]

of truth and is the foe of every educational program committed to guarding, enlarging, and disseminating the funded knowledge of the human race.

To be sure, education cannot be entirely divorced from immediate ends and objectives. Yet there is a center of gravity in education which is not the center of gravity in propaganda. The spirit of education differs from that of propaganda. In some respects, as in other matters, it is a question of emphasis, but the emphasis is fundamental. The propagandist deliberately refuses to present with all the fairness that human fallibility will permit the other positions or points of view which enter into competition with his own. He places the interest of his group above all other interests. His temper is dogmatic, not inquiring or reasoning. He puts forward opinions as established facts and closes his mind to new truths incompatible with his ends. If education could perchance endorse any of his designs, it could not proceed in his spirit or follow his methods without violating its trust. By its inescapable obligations, it has other functions to discharge.

VII.

Conditions Requisite for the Discharge of Educational Obligations.

Taken in its fulness, education stands apart from the other public services, such as public works and public safety, and is distinguished by obligations of its own. It underlies and helps to sustain all public services. The schools furnish in the main the preliminary discipline upon which training for the services is based, and state universities provide technical instruction necessary for the discharge of professional duties. The schools and colleges disseminate knowledge pertaining to the sciences, arts, and crafts employed in every branch of administration. They distribute information and promote understanding respecting the services—information and understanding calculated to maintain the public support and cooperation which enable administrative division to function effectively. Education also supplies an ethical cement that helps to hold together the very civilization in which all services operate, upon which they depend for sustenance. American society could exist on some level of comfort and convenience without improved roads, electric lights, or sanitary codes; it did in the eighteenth century and at the same time demonstrated qualities of true greatness; but it cannot exist upon its present level or attain a higher level, with an illiterate and ignorant population dominated by low standards of taste, subsistence wants, and primitive conceptions of life.

School Administrators Need
Special Qualities.

When education is considered in terms purely administrative, distinctions from other services are likewise evident. The school boards and boards of college trustees
responsible for the general policies and the administration
of education have contacts with society and power over
individuals that are different from, and wider-reaching in
subtle consequences than those assigned, for instance, to a
government commission which regulates railway rates,
passes upon the trade practices of given industries, or
makes rules for transactions arising from workmen's com-
pensation laws. To emphasize this would be to repeat all
that has been said before. The school superintendent also
has duties not imposed on any other administrative officer.
Records and accounts he must keep or scrutinize; esti-
mates and reports he must prepare; and other functions of
administrative routine he must perform. In these respects
his responsibilities resemble those of administrative officers
in general; although his statistical statements represent dis-
tinct aspects of human life and aspirations, as well as
money, materials, buildings, and supplies. But the superintendent's obligations are more extensive.

Those of the health commissioner, the superintendent of
public works, the director of public welfare, and other administrative officers are not to be underestimated; but
their duties and contacts with society are limited and specialized. As head of a system in which all arts and sciences
are taught, the school administrator is called upon to possess knowledge and intellectual interests that are broader
than those of any one profession. Without this knowledge
and these interests he cannot act effectively as the channel
of communication between the school board and the

teachers who organize curricula and carry on instruction, to say nothing of taking the leadership expected of him in such matters. As head of the schools he is subject to impacts from nearly all the interests, good and bad, that operate in the community; not merely to those touching health, or public works, or the relief of dependents. Under his jurisdiction are children from practically all sections of the community; not merely those affected by specific regulations of a police, sanitary or industrial character. Literally nothing that goes on in the community is alien to him. The very nature of his office imposes peculiar duties upon him. It is not by speeches at political rallies or by public appearances that he discharges them; his work is in the domain of knowledge and aspiration; and often the less that is heard about it, the better it is done. If, legally speaking, the school superintendent is one administrator among many, the term is meaningless until the primary functions of education are brought into consideration. It is then that the unique characteristics of educational administration become evident and present the case for a special administrative relation to the general structure of government.

*Yet Education Is One among Many Branches
of a Growing Public Service—All
Involving Public Support.*

From the point of view of finance and administration, however, education is one among many public services associated with the rising standards of civilization. Communities demand better highways, more adequate water supplies, improved public health administration, hospitals, public works, and other technical utilities deemed essential to good living. Like education, these services have usually imposed burdens upon tax resources and have led not unnaturally to a certain competition among them for financial support.

Demand Has Arisen for More Centralized Control over All Divisions of Administration.

The pressure of the public services upon the community for revenues has been largely responsible for the rise and growth of a movement for budget reform and for the consolidation of all administrative agencies in a centralized system. Leaders in this movement call attention to the increase in expenditures rendered necessary by the expansion of public services. They point out that as the services have multiplied and outlays have strained the resources available, budget-making and the unification of agencies have become imperative. They insist that since resources are limited and curtailments in expenditures are demanded, all the services seeking places in the budget must be appraised as parts of a common program. Extremists among them propose to make educational administration a mere branch of the general administration, headed by a single political officer, and to treat the school budget as a mere division of the general budget. Besides urging these alterations in the position of the schools, they advocate a thoroughgoing centralization of accounting, purchasing, plant construction, and personnel administration.

Any Adaptations to Schemes of Centralization Are To Be Made within the Limits of Educational Objectives.

Educational administrators recognize the exigencies out of which the demand for efficiency and economy has sprung, and the community interests which they are designed to serve. Where it can be demonstrated that there are net advantages in the consolidation or coordination of administrative operations, it should be effected, in so far as the unique services of education are not thereby impaired. At all times there should be a free exchange of technical experiences and opinions in respect of common administrative processes throughout the entire government; and this exchange will be facilitated as the standards of competence and public responsibility are raised in all branches of government. But in these consultations and efforts in cooperation, school and college authorities are compelled by the obligations of their trusts to safeguard the fundamental nature of the educational function, and to point out with unceasing reiteration its primary and basic character, its intellectual and moral contributions to the maintenance of the society upon which all services depend for their existence and support. Whether it is a question of budget-making, the keeping of accounts, the selection of personnel, the purchase of supplies, or the design and construction of school buildings, the indubitable requirements of education call for fiscal and administrative distinctions fully adapted to the care and training of youth.

This does not mean that educational authorities are or should be indifferent to the demand that school budgets be made and school administration conducted with reference to the total financial situation of the community or of the larger areas to which they may be related. In the best of jurisdictions school budgets are prepared with a view to the requirements of the other services and the financial resources available to all. In these jurisdictions school authorities are well informed respecting the state of general revenues and expenditures and do give to appropriate budget-making officers, as well as to the public, complete information relative to school receipts and outlays. They also seek information on the general situation from fiscal officers and invite from other specially qualified persons and the public a consideration of the tentative educational budget before reaching final determinations. This best practice should be more widely extended. By such processes of developing information and suggestions, the advantages of economy and efficiency may be obtained without surrendering that degree of autonomy necessary to the discharge of educational obligations. Understandings of this character are the more readily effected where school superintendents are well prepared by training and experience for taking leadership in community affairs and for presenting to the public and its official representatives the school budget in terms of the human values covered by its items; and like demands may properly be made upon other administrative officials in their special fields. Herein seems to lie the hope for meeting the legitimate demands for efficiency and economy in general administration while safeguarding the fiduciary trust vested in educational authorities by the American system of government.

Settled Practice Accords a High Degree
of Administrative Freedom to
Education at All Levels.

The peculiar nature of education and its functions in society have been recognized by the sober judgment of the American people as expressed in constitutions and statutes. This judgment is revealed in many types of administrative authorities to which educational responsibilities are assigned by law. These vary, no doubt, from state to state, and region to region; but one fundamental principle underlies almost all of them. It is that authorities, state and local, in charge of the public schools and colleges are to stand apart from the executive and legislative branches of the government which respond annually, biennially, or quadrennially to the majority or plurality of votes cast in popular elections at the close of political campaigns.

The remoteness varies in degree. Members of the school board may be chosen by popular vote at a general or special election, and thus stand upon an independent basis. As a rule this independence in elective trustees is strengthened by renewing only a portion of the board at each election, thus assuring a certain continuity in policy. If the members are appointed by an executive authority alone, or in conjunction with the legislative branch or one house thereof, they are usually given longer terms and provision is made for overlapping tenures so that the political agents endowed with appointing power can seldom make a clean sweep of the officials in charge of education. Moreover, where general administrative control over the schools is vested in a board of some kind, practice often permits bi-partisan or multi-partisan representation. Frequently the school board is given an independent taxing power, within limits, and in such circumstances is not even subject to executive and legislative control in matters of finance or of educational policy in detail.

Other differences in methods and agencies of control have been developed for various levels and branches within the school system. The public elementary and secondary school systems, although creatures of the state, are ordinarily administered by district, municipal, or county boards of education. The colleges and universities which make up the states' systems of higher education are commonly controlled by appointed or elected boards of regents. Amid all this diversity of administrative machinery, however, a high degree of administrative freedom is generally provided not only for the local public school systems, but also for state educational administration, and for the agencies of higher education and research. The discussion here is to be interpreted in inclusive terms; "education," "teachers," and "schools" refer not merely to the elementary and secondary fields, but to the higher institutions of learning and research as well.

The Desire To Keep Education out of Partisan
Politics Is One of the Reasons for
Administrative Protection.

The removal of educational administration some degree from periodical turnovers in regular legislative and executive offices is no accident. Although it cannot be said that in the beginning our law-makers always had a positive philosophy of administrative independence for the schools, they early discerned a distinction between education and other public service functions. The idea of vesting public power in a board, as distinguished from a single elective or appointive officer, was, of course, no novelty in the middle period of American history, when the foundations of public education were securely laid. There were many American precedents in other departments of administration, especially where large powers in the determination of policy were assigned to public agencies.

If the nature of educational functions had not been sufficient to warrant the practice of resorting to boards, the desire to escape from the obvious evils of the spoils system and partisan squabbles, introduced wholesale in the Jacksonian era, might have effected that outcome. Indeed, in some cases, such as police and health administration, the board system was deliberately adopted with a view to making administration at least bi-partisan in con-

trol and direction. Whatever may have been the determining factor in the case of education, the administration
of the schools was early committed to boards and they
were assigned a high degree of independence in matters of
policy and finance.

Even Administrative Consolidation Recognizes the
Special Position of Education.

There has been, it is true, a decided reaction against the
confusion of independent boards, offices, and commissions
which Jacksonian democracy promoted. This reaction
has appeared in the consolidation of state and local administration in all parts of the Union. And it has been
assumed by some logicians that the concentration of
authority will and must continue until all public functions
are united and organized in hierarchical form, with a
single political executive at the top. Yet, as a matter of
fact, along with this powerful movement in the direction
of administrative unification, practices of another tendency have continued or developed, especially in connection with education.

Other Public Functions Are Provided with
Kindred Safeguards.

For example, from the very beginning of American
history a certain independence has been assigned to the
judiciary. Entirely apart from their function of passing
upon the constitutionality of statutes, judges deal with
vital matters of long-time interest, such as crime, civil
liberty, property rights, and domestic relations. Whatever may be the results of periodical elections, whatever
changes legislators may make in the civil and criminal law,
the new is connected with the old, and fundamental mat-

ters continue from decade to decade or develop slowly under the impact of forces not purely or even mainly political.

On such grounds, judges of superior courts are given life terms, or long terms, and seldom is an entire bench renewed at a single election. There is also a tendency to make the election of judges non-partisan, by the removal of party symbols and designations from the ballot in judicial elections. Moreover, positive restrictions are placed upon the removal of judges by political authorities. By and large, the judgment of the American people runs against throwing the punishment of crime, the granting of divorces, and the adjudication of personal relations into the turmoil of annual or biennial elections.

The removal of public agencies some degree from immediate political turnovers has not been confined to the judiciary. Many branches of federal and state administration, especially boards and commissions, have been given a special position in the frame of government. This is particularly true of agencies that have semi-legislative and semi-judicial, as well as administrative functions. Striking examples are furnished by the Interstate Commerce Commission, the Federal Power Commission, and the Federal Trade Commission. Members of these bodies, though appointed by the President and Senate, are given long terms. Their tenures are made overlapping, so that a certain continuity of competence is assured; and, in the ordinary course, single popular elections do not make drastic changes in the personnel. In addition, the removal power of the President is hedged about by restrictions, with a view to attenuating the force of mere partisanship.

There is basic work that must go on in society whatever the cast of the party thought and the direction of particular decisions at the polls. With the growth of technological functions in economy and government, this basic work expands and the dependence of society upon the competence employed in it increases. All these things are now recognized by law, incorporated in practice, and sustained by an informed public opinion.

As a matter of fact, in many departments of government where the executive has free appointing and removal power, competence, tenure, and promotion are safeguarded by practice, for reasons similar to those applied by law in many instances. A searching study of Federal usage in these matters of personnel shows that relatively few of the divisions and bureaus, about one-fifth of the total number, are purely political, in that the heads are likely to be ousted with each party turnover. Nearly all the technical divisions—entomology, plant industry, forestry, reclamation, chemistry, and public roads, for example—are now generally established on the merit basis. The worst spoilsman in Federal politics would not put an untrained real estate agent in charge of research in fixed nitrogen. If he were so inclined, the pressure of civic and professional associations, organized outside the Government, would place barriers in his way. The most ardent partisanship must recognize the expediency, if not the social need, of competence in technical and professional branches of the government. Even states and municipalities which have no civil service laws take some account of this reality by safeguarding competence in carrying on the basic functions of government.

Autonomy Is in Keeping with
Democratic Principles.

In all this there is no denial of democracy. No public agencies, no public policies, are placed beyond the reach of the popular verdict as delivered in due course. Democracy requires that the judgment of the people must prevail, but American institutions are designed to assure that in matters fundamental the popular judgment be matured. In other words, they do not place all rights and obligations of life, liberty, and economy at the disposal of the majority or plurality which carries a single election for political officers. Such rights are not absolute, nor are they indefensible against government for all time. No public officer or private person enjoys privileges forever beyond the sovereignty of the seasoned popular verdict. Legal safeguards, tenure, and independence, of whatever kind or degree, are intended to serve, not to block, the deliberative processes of democracy and to guarantee the competent discharge of its primary functions. The principle is not to be employed as a subterfuge. It is entitled to more than lip service. It is so fundamental to the future of democratic society that it must be respected, maintained, and defended, if a way is to be steered between government by plebiscite and government by privilege, whether newly usurped or entrenched in tradition and prescription.

It is within an institutional setting which assures a certain competence and continuity of administration that education has also been assigned a high degree of independence. This independence is no accident of politics and law; it is, at least in a large measure, the result of deliberate policy, adopted with reference to the broad purposes of education and defended on positive grounds. Yet the autonomy so guaranteed does not cut education off from society, or from the long-run judgments of the electorate. The protection afforded, such as it is, merely runs against the pressure of active and vociferous minorities, and to some extent against particular majorities which win control of the executive and legislative departments at particular moments on issues other than those of education. In due course the deliberate opinion of the community prevails in educational administration, as far as general policy goes; but even community judgment cannot overturn the knowledge which education is pledged to cherish and disseminate, without destroying education.

There Are Special Grounds for Vigorously Supporting Educational Independence.

But general principles are not enough. In view of the pressures brought upon the schools by organized minorities, in view of recent legislation questioning the integrity and loyalty of teachers, in view of recent political interference with professional appointments and dismissals, in view of the demand that education be placed immediately under the financial control of executive and legislative authorities, it is necessary to go into details. Why does public policy assign a high degree of independence to education?

Scientific Instruction Is Independent of Politics.

1. With respect to technical and scientific subjects of instruction in the schools, especially those related to the practical arts, education is in fact independent of political turnovers at the polls. This rule applies to mathematics, the natural sciences, and many elements of studies less exact in nature. The swings of popular majorities do not affect the validity of the multiplication table. The law of gravitation operates under Democratic as well as Republican or Socialist administrations. The conjugation of English and Spanish verbs is not ousted by an incoming party fresh from victory. If in a moment of excitement

a legislature should order the schools to teach that the world is flat, educational administration cannot obey, if it is to be loyal to knowledge and truth. Where it is necessary to formulate a curriculum adapted to the demands of the practical arts or community needs of any kind, the selections to be made, the methods to be adopted, and the organization to be effected must be entrusted to those having technical competence, if the very ends of instruction are not to be defeated. However able political executives and legislatures may be, they can do no more than lay down general principles of educational policy and must entrust specifications to educational authorities.

The Humanities Have Their Independent Imperatives.

2. In the domain of the humanities—literature, the fine arts, economics, political science, and sociology, for example—the prescriptions of the subject matter are less exact than in languages and the natural sciences; but even in this domain there are immense bodies of authentic and exact knowledge which competence and loyalty to truth must take into the reckoning. Even to enumerate them requires an encyclopedia; for instance, the *Encyclopedia of the Social Sciences*. But illustration may be given. The prices of commodities, the wages of labor, and the costs of industrial insurance are not accidents, wholly subject to legislative fiat, irrespective of prevailing conditions. If they were, the Congress of the United States, or at all events a sovereign constitutional body could, by mere resolution, make everybody rich.

In human affairs, no less than in the astro-physical universe, there are some necessities by which even sovereign political force is limited. Although these necessities are not as clear and positive as in the physical world, political policy must take account of them and accept their requirements, at least in the long run. Competence has not yet reduced them to an exact science, but competence alone is fitted to explore and set forth their boundaries. Hence it must be said in the broad field of the humanities, where differences of opinion do appear, there are many findings sustained by the general consensus of competence. These findings do not dictate policy to political authorities, but they do set limits to the operations, methods, and results of policy. For this reason even partisanship must allow a high degree of liberty to inquiry and teaching in the humanities, unless it is totally indifferent to the outcomes of its own determinations. Although it is difficult to make this as clear to the heedless as the exigencies of the multiplication table, intelligence is fully aware of it, at least in sober moments.

The Teaching of Controversial Questions Calls for Judicial Prerogatives.

3. Into cultural subjects, such as history and economics, new ideas, or ideas foreign to the accepted thought and practice of the community, inevitably come, unless the subjects are deliberately distorted. For example, it is impossible to teach European history as truth without considering the diverse types of political, social, and economic theory and practice which have appeared in that history as fact. To state and describe those theories and practices with exactness and balance requires expertness of a high order and a scientific spirit foreign to the passionate disputes of partisan debate. Not even the ablest student of the subject will claim infallibility or the possession of "the whole truth." But certainly the informed and disciplined

mind can come nearer to the ideal type of fair and balanced instruction in such difficult subjects than the uninformed mind inflamed by partisan or sectarian passions.

This is no "academic" matter. What happens when politicians attempt to determine in detail the teaching of the social studies is illustrated by the controversy which arose in Washington, D. C., in 1935. By a rider attached to the District of Columbia Appropriation Bill in 1935 Congress provided: "Hereafter no part of any appropriation for the public schools shall be available for the payment of any person teaching or advocating communism." In response to a request for an interpretation presented by the school board, the corporation counsel held, first, that "teaching or advocating communism" meant "favoring" communism, and, secondly, that communism might be explained under the terms of the law. Under pressure from organized minorities, the Comptroller General made a ruling which implied that even a reference to communism might imperil the position of teachers in the District of Columbia schools.

At all events the outcome of the law and the rulings was a bitter conflict which embarrassed the school board, the superintendent, the teachers, and the citizens of the District of Columbia and brought repercussions throughout the country. Nor was the contest limited to passionate debates in Congress, the press, the public forums. Not content with the law and the rulings, the chief sponsor of the Act set himself up as an authority on all the social studies, and subjected the superintendent and teachers to an examination in the correct and permissible presentation of these subjects in the District schools. The nature of this layman's excursion into educational policy and the teaching of the social sciences is set forth at length, for the edification of the nation, in the *Hearings* on the District of Columbia Appropriation Bill, 1936, pp. 519-787.

Here is a perfect exhibition of the events to be expected when busy politicians, unacquainted with the complexities of education, invade the autonomy of the school board and undertake to prescribe subjects and methods of instruction in detail. The retirement of the chief troublemaker from Congress by his constituents could not atone for the turmoil created in the District schools, remove the stings of his indignities and misrepresentations, or immediately restore the conditions necessary for the competent and impartial administration of education.

Preparation for Citizenship Transcends
All Partisan Limits.

4. There are wider and more secure reasons for a high degree of educational autonomy than the exigencies of mere competent instruction in the natural sciences and the social studies. They lie in the processes of democratic government itself. These processes, as already indicated, involve freedom of citizens to propose measures of government, liberty of discussion, unawed and unbought decisions on policies and measures, and continuous reexamination and appraisal of their results. These processes call for knowledge and an attitude of mind which are indispensable to the endurance of democracy. To acquire, preserve, and disseminate such knowledge is a primary function of education. It is likewise the bounden duty of education to give that mental training which prepares the people for discussion in an informed and equitable spirit, and for the acceptance of popular decisions without resort to force, "the parent of despotism."

In the higher ranges of public education, issues of current society must come into instruction unless it is to be sterile and false to life. Here under the direction of trained and competent teachers pupils may be taught to look all around modern problems, to examine the points of view from which discussion proceeds, to acquire exact knowledge, to learn the assumptions on which decisions depend, and to develop that even temper so necessary to the preservation of democratic institutions. When the processes and ends of our democratic society are placed above the exigencies of partisan politics and the immediate advantages of power, then it becomes evident that education as a safeguard and preparation for democratic living must not be subjected every hour and in every way to the unrestrained control of men and women lifted into political office for a brief term by the fortunes of campaigns and elections.

To Education Are Entrusted Enduring Interests and Values.

5. Beyond this argument it seems impossible to go. Yet one more step seems necessary. Owing to the nature of popular usage, there is danger that the term *democratic society* be taken too narrowly, in a mere political sense. Society is more than politics. It embraces all culture. And democracy implies the widest possible diffusion of culture and all the means essential to the good life. Committed by its historical and immediate obligations to cherishing and advancing the funded wisdom, knowledge, and aspirations of the race, education carries responsibilities which outrun the fortunes of annual, biennial, or quadrennial elections, the ups and downs of parties, the twists and turns of public opinion. In a literal sense, education

is rooted in eternity, despite its proper affiliation with temporal events. It is concerned with all the humane interests which shape society, government, and public policies, and give richness to individual life. The very nature of such obligations and undertakings accord to education in the United States a special position among the administrative services of government.

But Foes of Educational Autonomy Are Abroad in the Land.

Yet the loyalty and competence of teachers are attacked by special legislation imposing oaths on them and forbidding them to "teach" certain topics. As far as the oath to support the Constitution of the United States and the State is concerned, little objection seems to lie on the surface of things. Are not the employees of the schools public officers? Are not public officers required to take an oath of office? If resort is had to technicalities, then note must be taken of the fact that most employees in the schools are not public officers in the legal sense. They belong to the great body of civil servants of whom oaths are not ordinarily required. Subordinate employees in engineering, health, and other professional services are employees, not public officers, and oaths are not exacted of them. Thus to impose oaths on all teachers, and to forbid the teaching of subjects belonging of right to education, is in fact to single teachers out as a class and to assume the existence of disloyalty to country and to knowledge in their ranks. It also assumes that anyone who is disloyal in fact will be deterred from taking the oath, or will be transformed by the oath into a loyal citizen.

They Are Aided by Sensational Journalism.

But opposition to special oaths for teachers does not rest on technical grounds. It is not the mere nature of the oath in itself that has awakened powerful protests. It is the auspices under which such legislation has been promoted and driven through legislatures that give cause for alarm. A survey of recent history shows that in nearly every case the oath law is the outcome of pressure brought to bear upon the legislature by organized minorities, aided and abetted by the propaganda of sensational newspapers. The sincerity of many citizens who have taken part in this agitation is conceded, but concerning the original animus and the driving force behind it there can be no doubt.

It was sponsored and financed by sensational journalism. And American teachers have learned from bitter experience that sensational journalism, by featuring crime, scandal, and sex perversions, has been and still is the foe of everything that is finest in civilization, of everything which education is under obligation to nourish and cherish. Nor can it be doubted that many agitators who have been associated with the sensational press in its campaign against the schools are open foes of that freedom of inquiry and discussion guaranteed by our constitutions—that liberty absolutely indispensable to democratic processes and to the guardianship and promotion of learning. Such are the grounds on which reasoned opposition to oath legislation rests.

And They Are Often Motivated by Other Interests.

Moreover, an examination of the literature and testimony offered in support of oath legislation shows that its proponents are often zealously engaged in imposing their views of social policy upon teachers, if apparently interested in sustaining the integrity of education. Among them are found advocates of military training in the schools, of universal military service, of the sales tax as a means of raising public revenues, of measures denying to citizens rights guaranteed to them by their constitutions, and of kindred projects. Military training in the schools, universal military service, and sales taxes, for example, may properly be debated on their merits. Even propositions to deprive citizens of rights now guaranteed by their constitutions are not beyond the bounds of discussion. But support of these measures is not imposed upon teachers by public law. Even teachers who approve them on their merits are under obligation, oath or no oath, to treat them as mere proposals under consideration, and to distinguish them from settled mandates standing on the same footing as constitutions. Whatever their attitude to such measures may be, they must in loyalty to truth oppose every effort to identify these schemes with the existing Constitution of the United States or of any state, or with the necessary spirit of American institutions. This is not partisanship. It is a command of knowledge and of fundamental law. To hold otherwise is to abandon both the letter and spirit of education and to assume that truth is of no importance in the affairs of mankind.

The Counter Case for Educational Values Has the Powerful Support of National Leaders.

The case against this assault on the integrity of education was powerfully, yet simply, stated by Governor Alfred M. Landon in his address at Chautauqua on August 24, 1936. "If education is to realize its true goal," he said, "it cannot confine itself to an academic discussion of life

—it must become a part of life itself. I believe that education is making a great contribution to the solution of our difficulties. It is creating increased interest and stimulating discussion. Letting every man have his say is the constitutional method of solving our problems. Why should we make teaching a suspect profession, by making our teachers take a special oath? The self-sacrifice and devotion of our teachers is one of the finest examples of public service. I believe that a teacher has a right to the same freedom of speech in expressing his political, social or religious convictions as any other citizen. And I believe that a teacher has the same right to work for the accomplishment of his political and social ideals as any other citizen."

Speaking at Harvard University later in the year, President Roosevelt reinforced the same principles of liberty in education. "In this day of modern witch-burning," he said, "when freedom of thought has been exiled from many lands, it is the part of Harvard and America to stand for freedom of the human mind and to carry the torch of truth. The truth is great and will prevail. For centuries that grand old saying has been a rock of support to persecuted men. But it depends on men's tolerance, self-restraint and devotion to freedom, not only for themselves but also for others, whether the truth will prevail through free research, free discussion, and free intercourse of civilized men, or will prevail only after suppression and suffering—when none cares whether it prevails or not. . . . To pay ardent reverence to the past but to recognize no less the direction of the future; to understand philosophies we do not accept and hopes we find it difficult to share; to account the services of mankind the highest ambition a man can follow, and to know that there is no calling so humble that it cannot be instinct with that ambition; never to be indifferent to what may affect our neighbors; always, as Coleridge said, to put truth in the first place and not in the second; these I would affirm are the qualities by which the 'real' is to be distinguished from the 'nominal' scholar."

Educational Liberty Has Constitutional Foundation.

Governor Landon and President Roosevelt spoke with authority, out of clear knowledge of American institutions and in the spirit of educational liberties. The Constitution of the United States and the fundamental law of each state guarantee the freedom of inquiry and discussion which education is under obligation to preserve and cherish. That is not all. These constitutions also make provisions for changes which eventuate from freedom of inquiry and discussion; besides giving a wide latitude for operations of policy within the limits of existing constitutional law. In common with all other citizens, teachers are under obligation to respect the law; but in common with all other citizens they must recognize that changes in the law are constantly before the public for consideration. If they observe the dictates of truth when they teach the subjects touching government, economy, and society, they are compelled to present fairly and squarely changes which have been made, great issues of change now pending, and the underlying assumptions by which they are to be determined. An oath to support a constitution does not impose an obligation to condemn and resist changes in it; such an oath carries with it an express obligation to support provisions which authorize alterations. This is obvious enough to seem banal, but confusion in public opinion requires restatement.

School Authorities Have the Obligation
To Sustain Educational Liberty.

In respect of legislative measures imposing upon schools the duty to teach certain subjects or to refrain from teaching them, other considerations prevail. The right of political authorities, within constitutional limits, and of the electorate through proper process, to require the teaching of some subjects and the exclusion of others is beyond question. Yet it is the duty of educational authorities to scrutinize ordinary legislative acts with reference to constitutionality. Surely the guardians of education have the same right as any interested private party to challenge in the courts any and all infringements of constitutional guarantees. By the very nature of the duties committed to them, they are especially obligated to do so. An individual may sacrifice a right, but public authorities, charged with fiduciary responsibilities, cannot do it without betraying their trust. No school board is bound to obey a legislative act that is judged by proper legal authority to violate the constitution under which it operates.

Where a duty is legally and properly imposed upon educational authorities, they are compelled to adjust the discharge of that duty to all the responsibilities entrusted to them by law. Any other conception would make the whole curriculum a sport of passing legislative majorities. To confer upon a legislator or an executive in charge of other matters the power to prescribe minute rules for education is to declare school boards, superintendents, and teachers unworthy of their office and to shake the confidence of pupils in the integrity of instruction.

All These Circumstances Reinforce the Need
of Legal Protection for Education.

Thus, disturbing events bring forcibly to the foreground the necessity for assuring to educational authorities throughout the entire school system a wide range of freedom in the determination of policies and the conduct of the schools. They are not entitled to, and do not seek, a position of impregnable irresponsibility against society or its matured judgments. They do not deny the validity of the claim that community budgets must be balanced, by curtailments if necessary, in time of stress. They accept the broad principle of democratic control. It is against the ravages of transitory politicians engaged in mere inquisitorial expeditions that they demand protection. They object to having teaching positions in schools and universities turned into the spoils of office, with continuous unsettlements and turnovers from election to election. They protest against allowing any legislative or administrative authority, chosen for other purposes and mainly engrossed in other business, to intervene at will in educational administration, to threaten college presidents, superintendents, and teachers with reprisals, to upset carefully arranged curricula for petty reasons, to dictate the purchase of books and materials, to locate school buildings with respect to real estate projects, and otherwise to subject the schools to passing tempers and the demands of private interests. In stating their position, school authorities merely say that those responsible for educational policies and administration should be in fact responsible, should have powers commensurate with their duties, and should be immune against sporadic raids by men who are not responsible. In so contending they simply assert a fundamental principle of democracy and sound administration.

As a unique form of public service, having obligations different from and transcending other services, education must insist upon measures of law designed to assure it that form of autonomy in which it can best discharge its particular functions.

To Legal Safeguards Must Be Added
Safeguards of the Spirit.

Legal rules, however, are not enough. Institutions of government must be sustained and supplemented by a determined spirit and by the efforts of individuals and associations united on constructive principles. Educators, no more than citizens at large, can expect to enjoy liberty without deserving it, by the mere fact of their existence. Human affairs do not run that way. Authorities in charge of the schools—boards, administrators, and teachers alike —and citizens desirous of protecting the educational trust against narrow views and passing tempers are themselves under obligation to weight their case with values beyond debate. They must be on guard against their own special interests and inquire into their own motives. It is not enough for them to assert privileges and to criticize in general terms political officers who seek economy and efficiency in government, or who put forward educational policies for public approval. The issue is not one of prescriptive right against power. It is rather one of established and demonstrated educational services against a short-sighted conception of public policies. So cherished and defended, education may confidently look forward to securing from society that autonomy and economic support to which it is entitled on its merits.

And Eternal Vigilance Is Necessary.

It may be said that these alarms are without warrant and that these principles are obviously taken for granted. Yet we have been duly instructed that eternal vigilance is the price of liberty. We know that the schools have been and are subjected to the pressures of powerful minorities, seeking to impose their policies, not only by law, but also by threats of reprisals. We see upon our statute books an increasing volume of legislation dictating the substance of education and the procedures to be followed in the classroom. We see competent teachers, principals, state superintendents, and university presidents dismissed for partisan or factional motives that threaten the very integrity of learning. To what lengths this tendency may go, we have no way of knowing. But concerning the animus and logic of some measures and actions there can be no doubt. Exact knowledge of current forces and movements is sufficient to forewarn us. The way to insure the integrity of education is to be on guard against violations and to adopt practices designed to preserve it against dissensions within and attacks from without. No golden road is open to us but experience suggests possible procedures. In providing the conditions necessary to the discharge of their obligations, educational authorities may find guidance in the efforts of constitution-makers to combine liberty with authority, and progress with security.

This Vigilance Calls for Perfecting the Constitution of Self-Government for Education.

Despite numerous conflicts over "autonomy of the schools" and "freedom of teaching," few school authorities have worked out for their own guidance a statement of

[127]

the fundamental principles to be employed in resolving such difficulties. Yet in a collective view of the best practices now prevailing, we can see the broad outlines of a constitution of self-government in education already taking form. Here, in the best practices, are defined the broad purposes of education and the powers of the agencies authorized to carry them into effect. The duties and rights of school boards, administrators, and teachers in general and in particular are set forth. Rules controlling the relations of school authorities to other branches of the government, to the public, to parents, to superintendents, and to teachers are laid down. The obligations of teachers and pupils in classroom exercises, especially those involving controversial issues, are clarified. Agencies and procedures for the adjudication of differences of opinion respecting rights and duties have been instituted. It remains for us to unite the fragments, to generalize the best achievements, to enlarge upon and illuminate them, and to project for the future an educational philosophy and practice to which men and women of good-will may repair, trusting that events beyond the horizon will justify, continue, and improve the work thus far advanced.

The Demand for More Enlightenment and Greater Effort Is Here.

Many obstacles, no doubt, lie in the way of realizing the ideals and discharging the admitted obligations of education. The task places a heavy strain on the competence and the qualities of administrators and teachers; and the school is merely one of the many agencies concerned with education in its widest sense. Such contentions are to be readily conceded. The answer, however, is not to lower the objectives established, to seek an easier way, or to narrow education to the routine of the common denominator in the profession. The ideals are clearly before us, in the heritage of education and in the prescriptions of its leaders from antiquity to our own times. They are by no means the peculiar possession of public education; yet public education is bound to cherish and expound them. The responsibilities are likewise before us, in experiences evident even to the heedless. That the home, the church, the press, the radio, and private institutions also share the ideals and the responsibilities is recognized and must be emphasized. But in no way does this fact diminish the burdens of the public schools in their sphere. The degree to which administrators and teachers now fall below the highest standards set for them measures the urgency of the command that they enrich their own intellectual and spiritual resources, subject themselves to a more exacting discipline, and more abundantly deserve the public support through which education can attain its ideals and discharge its obligations.